MURDER A CIGARETTE

Ralph Harris & Judith Hatton

Foreword by W.F. Deedes

Duckworth

First published in 1998 by
Gerald Duckworth & Co. Ltd.
61 Frith Street
London W1V 5TA
Tel: 0171 434 4242
Fax: 0171 434 4420
Email: duckworth-publishers.co.uk

ISBN 0 7156 2891 7

A catalogue record for this book is available
from the British Library.

Printed and bound in Great Britain by
Redwood Books Ltd, Trowbridge

Contents

Foreword

Lord Deedes PC, MC

I grow uneasy about our attitude to smokers. My uneasiness increases every time I see a young woman furtively drawing on a cigarette in the doorway of her office. She has the look of a woman who has just strangled her pet cat in a fit of rage and feels thoroughly ashamed of herself.

She is a symbol of something that has gone badly wrong. This normally level-headed race has been persuaded that to be in the presence of someone who likes cigarettes is the equivalent of being dangerously close to someone with a contagious disease.

It is our loss of level-headedness that troubles me most. We have allowed a lot of extremely doubtful propaganda to create panic when someone lights up in our presence. This is not a healthy state of affairs. If we are going to believe everything the anti-smoking lobby tells us, whom shall we have the strength of mind to disbelieve?

Declaring an interest, I smoked until the age of around 70. I gave it up because I reckoned that smoking increased my liability to bronchitis after a cold. Not everyone is affected that way, but I was. Smoking can lead to respiratory problems, just as drinking can lead to liver problems. (I have not given up drinking!)

So people are entitled to tell you politely that it is better for your health not to smoke or to drink alcohol. But both indulgences have throughout my long life been a matter of individual choice; and it is imperative that they so remain.

We have reached a point when it calls for a certain amount of courage to offer any sort of defence for smokers. On that account I salute both the authors of this book, Judith Hatton and Ralph Harris.

When I first knew Ralph, he was preaching, as director of the

Institute of Economic Affairs, the virtues of the free market. There were many who thought he should be burned at the stake for such heresy. Today most of the world, including our own Labour Party, accept that he was right.

Now, in company with Judith Hatton, he is preaching the gospel of tolerance. And because that is indispensable to every free society, sooner or later he will be proved right again.

July 1998   W.F. Deedes

Introduction

Puffers versus fumers

Perhaps I should make clear at the outset that nothing written here is intended to encourage adults, let alone children, to take up smoking. While we warmly welcome readers who are fellow-smokers, we have good reason to wish our non-smoking readers well and hope they are managing to get along calmly and contentedly with their lives without the solace we have both derived from our freely chosen indulgence. So long as they are broadly at ease, they will be less likely to sympathise with those sour prohibitionists who appear driven to vent their evident unhappiness on long-suffering smokers. That, indeed, is our best hope in writing this short book: not to win converts for smoking, but to justify a return to the once-famed British tolerance. Our method is to seek conscientiously to separate fact and logic from fiction and emotion in the great debate on the right of free citizens to smoke – always with courtesy and consideration for others, but untrammelled by needless coercion or constriction.

Choice or 'addiction'?

Judith Hatton and I must at least be given credit for knowing something of what we are talking about – quite apart from our close association with the leading European smokers' rights group, widely known as FOREST (Freedom Organisation for the Right to Enjoy Smoking Tobacco). Between us, we have smoked our cigarettes and pipes, respectively, contentedly and more or less continuously for well over a century. We can vouch that it has helped us through times of severe shocks, more frequent periods of stress and occasional episodes of loneliness. More generally smoking has helped us to enjoy a full share of conviviality and zest in busy lives.

When our presumed betters mock us as addicts, I would enquire when they last heard of a smoker mugging an old lady to get money for the next packet of cigarettes? If they persist, I would in the same spirit make a clean breast of it, plead guilty and ask for several other charges to be taken into account, including a life-long addiction to tea and coffee (each at least three times a day) porridge, bananas, lamb cutlets, and more recently to crunchy french bread, cheese, red wine and whisky (with ice and water, please). I am tempted to suggest at the outset that a moment's silence might be in order while readers ponder their own favourite 'addictions'.

More seriously, I must warn that our critics deliberately throw this word around to undermine the argument that smoking is no more than an exercise of free choice. What sort of free choice is it, they sneer, if weak-willed smokers are pathetically trapped in the vice of some overpowering compulsion? The short answer is that millions have felt driven, however reluctantly, to give up smoking without anything like the 'cold turkey' withdrawal symptoms that haunt former drug addicts – though often with unwelcome consequences for their waistlines. The fact that freedom of choice requires individuals to select their own preferred combination of pleasure and pain – in consumption or abstention, employment or retirement, even marriage or divorce – does not justify paternalists belittling free will and seeking to impose their 'superior' values on other adult men and women.

The chairman of the British Medical Association, Dr (now Sir) Sandy Macara, was reported in the *Western Daily Press* (September 1996) as saying:

> I don't accept that smokers are truly addicted to tobacco, I think they have a habit .... Smokers could stop tomorrow – no today – if they really wanted to.

Whether or not it got him into hot water, he later blamed the paper for omitting a passage about longer-run effects on dependency. I nevertheless take my stand with the world-famed psychologist and geneticist, the late Professor Hans Eysenck, that the word 'addiction' has no precise meaning and should not be bandied about as though it had, least of all by scientists. If challenged, I would at a pinch brandish the measured verdict on tobacco of the American Psychiatric Association:

> ... there is no impairment in social or occupational functioning as an immediate and direct consequence of its use.

But 'no impairment'? Along with many smoking friends, I would emphatically claim a positive improvement. Indeed, despite my lifelong addiction to consumer choice, I remain rather sad for those who have been nagged into forsaking the comforting embrace of Lady Nicotine.

Burden on the NHS?

To return to the two authors. For the statistically minded, my calculator puts our joint consumption of tobacco over our lifetimes – to date – at between 10 and 12 cwt, certainly more than half a ton, in the process adding significantly to employment and national income at home and abroad, not least in the local economy where we smokers remain a vital life-line for many corner shops. Even with my pipe at hand to steady my nerves, I hesitate to guess how much I have paid in sumptuary taxes over the years. It's not only non-smokers who might be astonished to learn that of the £2.80 paid for 20 cigarettes of a cheaper brand after the 1998 Budget, £2.44 goes to the government in tobacco duty, ad valorem tax and VAT. That is not far short of a 90% tax-take.

Come to think of it, as an economist – now happily recuperating in retirement – this issue of cost might be a good place to start on our voyage of rediscovering tolerance. It was, after all, a most blatant economic deception in the endlessly shifting statistical battle on smoking that first strengthened my dawning suspicion that even the high priests of the anti-smoking crusade would allow their obsession with health to distort their 'scientific' advocacy. Thus an assertion, repeated monotonously by spokesmen for tax-financed Action on Smoking and Health (ASH) and their acolytes in Parliament, was that in 1993 treatment of so-called 'smoking-related diseases' cost the NHS £610 million a year, recently mysteriously raised to between £1.4 and 1.7 billion a year. Such dubious, question-begging figures have been published periodically by the myopic missionaries of the Health Education Authority (HEA) and were used to show that, on top of all their other sins, smokers were a burden on the community, such as might even justify refusal by doctors to treat their 'self-inflicted' diseases.

We have heard less of this wild charge since its perpetrators discovered that FOREST was on their track with the simple truth that against any such phantom costs (see below), the taxes on tobacco now bring into the Exchequer around £10 billion (i.e. £10,000,000,000) a year, which is approaching a quarter of the escalating cost of the NHS. As for accusing smokers of 'self-inflicted diseases', it was the fearless *Times* columnist, Matthew Parris, who threw back the challenge:

> Your average *Guardian* reader would be horrified by any suggestion that someone who picked up HIV through unprotected sex had only himself to blame. Yet confront the liberal conscience with a smoker who has contracted lung cancer and 'serves him right' will lie just beneath the surface.

Yet smokers turn out to be a benefit rather than a burden on their fellow taxpayers, even more so if they obligingly die early and save government the cost of their pensions and the expensive medical treatments for diseases of the elderly. It follows that the practical question for the stop smoking (SS) brigade to answer is this: How would the Chancellor fill the £10 billion hole in his budget if the crusade succeeded in extinguishing the last cigarette and pipe? Our tormentors might heed the example of the London School of Economics professor Frank Paish who – though himself a non-smoker – always carried a box of matches ready to light his colleagues' cigarettes. He explained it was the least he could do in return for all the extra taxes they paid!

For the innocent reader who conscientiously wants to know what to believe, I would pose two more searching questions. First, if the health case is so powerful, how come such an obviously spurious financial argument could ever have been pressed into service against smokers? Secondly, should we take at face value other statistics which come from the same obsessive adversaries?

Lordly capers – enter the 'fumers'

Whatever your view about the hereditary aristocracy – or about the aristocratic tastes of a certain non-hereditary Lord Chancellor – you might share the broadly accurate view of what I like to call the 'Upper House' as a little aloof from the vulgar partisan bickering typical of elected assemblies. Life peers in particular mostly have fewer personal or political axes to grind and no troublesome constituents to placate. They also tend to be, shall we say delicately, senior citizens who have long wearied of the old party political claptrap and prefer to write their own speeches. Above all, the fabled reputation of the House of Lords as the best club in Britain is earned by the warm fellowship shared, irrespective of politics, by almost all but a few of the most determined loners and assorted eccentrics.

You might, therefore, expect that occasional debates on smoking would rise above the familiar recriminations and commonplace name-calling. Alas, it is grim testimony to the emotional force of the anti-smoking obsession that hopes of wiser or calmer counsels prevailing on this topic are not invariably fulfilled. Perhaps, after all, it's a tribute to the representativeness of the House of Lords that we include our share of those I hereby christen 'fumers'. I refer to non-smokers, often ex-smokers, for whom the mere mention of tobacco brings on all the symptoms of manic repression. In their presence, I am reminded that Adolf Hitler more or less invented the SS (stop smoking) brigade in the 1930s. In recounting a few examples, I shall refrain from naming names – if only out of respect for what I might call my peer group.

One of my most vivid memories since joining the Lords in 1979 is of a rather earnest non-smoking Baroness, married to an extremely amiable smoker who also happens to be a senior member of the Lords. What frenzy, I found myself wondering, could account for her taking up the time of other Lords, of Hansard writers and the usual quota of attendants, in an otherwise placid debate, to deplore her spouse's habit and to recite a humourless account of the trials of living with a smoker? All the while her husband was grimly pacing the corridors surrounding the Chamber until I tracked him down, brandished my pipe and led him off to finish his cigar over a reviving drink.

Then there was another life peeress, rather grander in style, despite taking the Labour whip, but no less deadly earnest in purpose, who revealed among her war aims the itch to curtail her colleagues' freedom to smoke. As though there were not already enough places around the House of Lords where smoking is prohibited, she moved behind the scenes to prevent its indulgence by peers in the main recreation rooms. That she did not succeed was thanks to opposition from a rather more formidable Tory peeress who not only smokes but positively smoulders on such encounters. However, what sticks in my mind was a private report of how the would-be abolitionist set about supporting her case by counting the cigarette ends deposited in ash-trays in the writing and television rooms! She was seen off this time and has since become a minister. But I fancy she will find time to keep a watch on those ashtrays. Or perhaps, with her educational background, she will engage a PhD student to monitor progress – just as the tax-financed HEA recently sponsored research by a Professor of Film Studies which included counting the smoking episodes on the big screen. It must be frustrating for the Professor to read the verdict of the playwright, John (now Sir John) Mortimer:

> I'm convinced that the large audiences for such works as *Brideshead* and *Jewel in the Crown* are partly drawn by the pleasure of watching leading characters puff away without guilt or inhibition.

It may be easy to airbrush out the cigarette or cigar in photos of famous people such as Presidents Roosevelt or Clinton, but how would Sherlock Holmes have solved all those crimes without his pipe?

A little later, early in 1997, sitting alone at my customary table in the section of the Lords' library where smoking is still permitted, I noticed a member I had never met entering in the distinctive garb of a bishop. What struck me was his suspicious manner. I watched him over my papers as he hesitantly made his way to the window and looked around anxiously before sliding his hand furtively beneath his robes and drawing out a packet of cigarettes. Even when he had lit one, he blew the smoke carefully towards the window and remained obviously ill at ease. So, puffing my pipe ostentatiously, I strolled across, introduced myself, and welcomed him as a possible new recruit for FOREST. With a natural charm and courtesy, he gently cut short further talk on the subject by waving his cigarette and explaining that a bishop had to be particularly careful of 'this kind of thing'. I took the first opportunity to look his name up in *Who's Who* and was deeply saddened to think so distinguished a churchman and scholar should be made to suffer the general sense of persecution.

So all smokers die young?

A much more seriously worrying episode arose in a debate on banning tobacco advertising in which I participated back in July 1994. My mild tormentor this time was another life peer and, alas, a fellow cross-bencher. He has the further distinction of being a physician with wide experience as consultant neurologist, university professor and much more, occupying four inches in *Who's Who*. I would add that he appears a man of unimpugnable integrity. It is therefore all the more notable that his anxiety to show smoking in the worst possible light led him, however unintentionally, to mislead their Lordships.

It arose in this way. Listening intently within a scalpel's thrust, I heard him recite the usual litany of the 'devastating effect on human health of smoking' – the number of deaths caused, the average years of life lost between the ages of 35 and 69, and the familiar, unending catalogue of unmitigated woes. When he sat down, I rose to ask him 'as a medical man' whether he denied any beneficial effects of smoking for some people, and referred to recent evidence that smokers over 60 had a better chance of avoiding Alzheimer's and Parkinson's Diseases. I concluded diffidently with a question; 'Does he not see any glimmer of that kind anywhere?' His reply was unequivocal and crushing:

> My Lords, no, I do not. In fact that evidence relating to Alzheimer's Disease and Parkinson's Disease has, I understand, been refuted subsequently.

Here was a confident, unequivocal reply. The only trouble is that it was wrong. Indeed, a few months earlier a prestigious specialist journal, the *New Scientist*, had revealed how the medical community was lining up with the anti-smoking lobby to suppress research showing the favourable effects of smoking on these two gruesome diseases, as well as on ulcerative colitis, rheumatoid arthritis and some cancers. The report even quoted researchers who accused funding bodies of failing to follow up promising leads from such studies, rather than acknowledge that nicotine could possibly have any beneficial effects. About the same time, one of the outstanding popular writers on all matters medical, Dr James Le Fanu, had reported in *The Times* on research showing the beneficial effects of smoking on various diseases, including a 50% reduced risk of developing Alzheimer's. (One study found that smokers are 70% less likely to suffer from it, and others suggested a 50% protection from Parkinson's.) The plot thickens. Reporting on the *New Scientist* findings, the *Evening Standard* wrote as follows:

> But London researchers say there are other explanations, such as the fact that smokers tend to die young, so are unlikely to develop diseases which affect the elderly.

It shows how far public opinion has been poisoned when a serious newspaper can publish a passage which assumes that not enough smokers survive into their 60s and 70s to permit a comparison between their health and that of a matched sample of non-smokers! Rather like the old saw about a peer who dreamt he was addressing the House of Lords and woke up to find that he was, I sometimes wonder if I should pause in filling my morning pipe to see if I live long enough to light it!

At the end of that Lords' debate, I scribbled a private note to the 'no, I do not' lord, expressing surprise at his flat denial. I am glad to relate that he promptly replied with an apology and acknowledged that, after checking the facts, he found he had inadvertently misled the House. For me, the deeper significance of this single incident goes far beyond an occasional, if convenient lapse by an unusually well-informed, scrupulous medical participant in a serious, on-the-record public debate. By commonsense extrapolation, it can be assumed that other less qualified and less scrupulous spokesmen, in a thousand unrecorded speeches, will routinely display a similar partial, wholly biased balance sheet of the relationship between smoking and health in all its ramifications.

To return to the relationship between smoking and health in all its ramifications: as we shall see later, 'cause of death' is an intrinsically complex question, where a true verdict would require attention to each individual's genetic inheritance, temperament, lifestyle, stress, location, socio-economic status, and many other variables, not least obesity and differences in diet which are commonly accepted to explain over a third of all cancer deaths.

The truth is that serious disease is seldom *caused* by a single factor. Indeed, for heart disease alone, modern medical research has identified several hundred 'risk factors' which may influence its development. As Judith Hatton explains, attempts by epidemiologists to measure statistical correlations, say, between smoking (or any other activity) and a particular disease, can seldom single out a firm *causal* relationship for the simple reason that the ubiquitous presence of 'confounding factors' leaves open too many alternative explanations.

'Smoking-related' survival?

Before finally leaving the House of Lords, I must bring to wider attention a question put down for written answer by Lord Stoddart of Swindon. Though not himself a smoker, he is perhaps the foremost champion on the Labour benches of individual freedom, including the right of adult voters to smoke. His long question, reported in the Lords' *Hansard* (24 July 1997), asked what were the 'so-called smoking-related diseases from which the government estimate 120,000 people [smokers] die each year' and how many died at what ages? The answer listed eight types of cancer and eight other diseases, including ischaemic heart disease, myocardial degeneration and pneumonia. Even a layman might at once surmise, correctly, that none of these diseases is confined to smokers. But a few of the startling facts that none would guess from all the propaganda run as follows.

- Of the total 630,000-odd deaths each year in the UK, almost two-thirds are from 'smoking-related diseases'.
- Over half all deaths of *non-smokers* are from 'smoking-related diseases'.

- Even in smokers, the majority of deaths from 'smoking-related diseases' are *not* considered to be due to their smoking.

The listed diseases turn out to be no more 'smoking-related' than a broken limb from a traffic accident can scrupulously be described, classified and publicised as a 'sports-related condition'. Further proof of misdescription is suggested by the answer in *Hansard* giving the age distribution, which shows that of about 400,000 estimated annual deaths from all 16 arbitrarily-chosen conditions, about 350,000 occur above the age of 65, and about 220,000 occur above the average expectation of life (74 for men and 79 for women). More simply, well over half of deaths from these diseases are suffered by smokers over 75. And bear in mind that all these confident, precise-looking estimates are subject to the unspoken margins of error in the data which Judith Hatton reveals in later chapters.

BR's smoke-screen

Readers will also learn from later chapters that there is no foundation whatever for fears that tobacco smoke can damage the health of non-smoking bystanders – so-called 'passive smoking'. But it can certainly damage their judgement by the affliction I have described as 'passive fuming'. Fumers are naturally thick on the ground in Westminster and at the EU Commission in Brussels. But away from politics, a prize example was provided by the British Rail persecutors of smokers on the Brighton line. The bare facts can be briefly told. At the end of 1992, on the brink of privatisation, BR announced an end to the long tradition whereby smokers and non-smokers were offered a choice of separate compartments. Out of the blue a ban on smoking was advertised on all trains throughout Network South-East. At once, FOREST protested on behalf of its members among the Brighton commuters, only to be rebuffed by BR claiming 'overwhelming support' from the travelling public on the basis of an opinion survey. When we asked to see the survey, BR pleaded commercial confidentiality until forced to come clean by a debate in the House of Lords.

In defiance of the ban, 60 to 100 regular commuters on the

morning and evening trains between Brighton and Victoria continued to smoke as before in the buffet carriage. Not until January 1995
did BR seek to enforce the ban by deploying its private railway police
to make an example of a particularly stubborn smoker named Peter
Boddington. Following prosecution and a £10 fine at Brighton
magistrates court, Mr Boddington at his own expense embarked
on a series of unsuccessful appeals, ending in defeat before the
House of Lords Court of Appeal in March 1998.

The grounds of appeal were complex but boiled down to challenging the legality and reasonableness of the by-law under which
BR *prohibited* smoking in the name of 'regulation'. However, the
case that could not apparently be deployed within the confines of
a court of law still seems to me in ordinary parlance a crushing
indictment of the special pleading to which even dull railway men
appear to be driven by the anti-smoking obsession.

In the first place, the claim of 'overwhelming support' for a
smoking ban turned out to have been drawn from a survey which
revealed among other findings that 61% of passengers on trains
where smoking was then allowed voted in favour of maintaining or
increasing existing provision. Secondly, the BR chairman failed to
consult the consultative committee whose well-established policy was
to recommend that 20% of carriages on journeys over an hour should
permit smoking. (The Brighton trains were made up of 12 carriages.)

Thirdly the chairman of BR then wrote to an MP as follows:

> We liaise carefully with statutorily constituted representatives of
> transport users and the respective proportions of smoking and
> non-smoking accommodation has been changed in response to
> regular consultations with them.

Fourthly, after giving a personal undertaking to consult fully
with FOREST before commissioning a new opinion survey, BR
went ahead without warning with a flawed telephone poll of 500
passengers (*including an undisclosed number on short 10, 20 and 30
minute journeys*) which, in response to a blatantly leading question
(referring to 'providing a cleaner, more pleasant environment
for all passengers'), predictably yielded a large majority (85%)
for the ban.

Finally, to confuse counsels even further, BR dared to claim that 'the research had the approval of FOREST, who were invited to contribute to the design of the questionnaire'.

'Oh, what a tangled web we weave....' And all this spin-doctoring was in aid of nothing more earth-shaking than striking a blow against 15 million fellow citizens who might wish space to carry on smoking! What renders the whole episode even more bizarre is that the persecution of Mr Boddington was continued after the BR 'fumers' had been taken over by Connex which was owned by a company from France – where more civilised tolerance is routinely extended on trains and elsewhere by provision for 'fumeurs' and 'non-fumeurs'. A small consolation, perhaps, is that Brighton has not yet followed Bournemouth in 'banning' smoking on the beaches and paying wardens to put up notices and enforce the 'respectful request', though without the power of railway police to impose fines or threaten imprisonment!

Is everything bad for you ...?

To prepare for the serious revelations to come, I would caution readers, like a jury, to clear their minds of the well-advertised preconceptions about dreaded tobacco as the 'usual suspect' for all imagined ills. As early as 1961, *Reader's Digest* popularised the quip: 'It is now proved beyond a doubt that smoking is one of the leading causes of – statistics.' But for the moment let us try to forget smoking.

If we are interested in specific statistics about other dangers, we can dip into *The Culture of Fear* by Dr Frank Furedi of the University of Kent. Starting from the risk of being struck by lightning or dying in a plane crash at 1 in 10 million (implying an average half a dozen deaths a year), he puts other possible risks (and implied deaths) as follows: 1 in a million (60 deaths) from eating beef; 1 in 500,000 (over 100 deaths) from a railway accident; 1 in 250,000 (over 200 deaths) from choking on food; 1 in 26,000 (2,000 deaths) from accidents at home; 1 in 8,000 from road accidents. Incidentally, Dr Furedi's own health warning is against 'safety [becoming] the secular religion of the Nineties' and society therefore becoming 'childlike and immature in the grip of fears, ever seeking reassurance from the nanny state.'

The political danger was anticipated a decade earlier by the broadcaster and former Labour MP, Brian Walden:

The desire for perfect safety is inexorably taking over the political agenda .... Everybody, everywhere, all the time, must be looked after, supervised and counselled lest they come to harm .... Already, a rising tide of social authoritarianism is apparent.

Since the 1960s, the craving for headlines has spawned almost incessant health scares, without relying on tobacco. It was, after all, the World Cancer Research Fund which announced that up to 40% of cancers could be avoided by a change in diet. So let us look a little more widely at some of the other dangers the restless media propagate at intervals between headlining the latest smoking scares. A glance at my drawer of press clippings over the past decade or so could easily convey the impression that everything you eat or drink or do can be bad for you. It's long been believed that fatty foods, sugar, sweets, salt, are high up as possible killers. But what are health freaks to do when they read that a student was killed by a 'veggie burger', that margarine is worse for the heart than butter, that a 'pinta milk a day' does after all protect against heart attack, that men with low cholesterol are more likely to commit suicide and that pickles may be linked to throat cancer?

Professor John Marks of Surrey University has taken special pleasure in teasing 'food-faddists in the muesli belt' for a great deal of nutritional nonsense, which he thinks is 'in danger of producing a generation of anorexics'. If he gets no press headlines for his sensible recommendation of 'a balanced diet containing a bit of everything, and everything in moderation', he would at least earn a cheer from the ever-steady Nigella Lawson who wrote in the *Evening Standard*:

What every sensible person knows is that moderation and pleasure are better guides to health and happiness than any amount of compulsive, self-punishing regimes.

I wonder what both would make of two recent reports under the headlines: HONEY CAN POISON YOUR BABY and YOUNG CHILDREN SHOW BIG INCREASE IN DEADLY PEANUT ALLERGY? I fancy they would chuckle at the latest headline from *The Times* (29 May 1998): POUR ON HEALTH WITH TOMATO SAUCE, which referred to researches showing reduced risk of heart attacks and prostate cancer among ketchup and pizza eaters. *The Times* rejoiced that 'food prigs have squashed tomatoes and stew on their faces!' Earlier, when research suggested that coffee might after all prove a mixed blessing, the tabloids competed with shock headlines: CAN COFFEE GIVE YOU CANCER? (*Mirror*), COFFEE & TEA AS BAD AS FAGS (*Sun*), PERIL IN THE PERCOLATOR (*Express*). The *Guardian* more sedately came up with: PICK-ME UP IS A LET DOWN. More recently, the *Telegraph* reported TOO MUCH COFFEE MAY DOUBLE THE RISK OF COT DEATH.

The temptation to switch to health drinks might be checked by a report in *Today* that slimming drinks put more than half teenage girls at risk from bone disease. A story in *The Times* that barbecued meat was linked to cancer enabled the partisan *Labour Briefing* to chant McDONALDS, McBASTARDS, McCANCER. *The Times*, again, reported on research that linked hot dogs with child leukaemia. For more sophisticated diners, the *Sunday Times* reported CANCER LINK TO CHINESE FOOD.

Although regular, moderate indulgence in red wine and whisky have recently come to be recommended by many doctors and health writers, alcohol abuse has increasingly been emphasised as dangerous. Even the heavyweight papers have competed for effect: ALCOHOL KILLS 500 A WEEK (*The Times*), DRINK DAMAGING HEALTH OF 1.4 MILLION (*Guardian*), DRINK CASES FILLING HOSPITAL BEDS (*Telegraph*), DYING FOR A DRINK (*Sunday Times*). So determined are the medical fraternity to take the pleasure out of drinking that if research doesn't support their warnings, its findings can simply be set aside. Thus in 1988, when a report by the International Agency for Research on Cancer (under the World Health Organisation) found that alcohol could not be proved to be carcinogenic (i.e. cancer causing), the authors concluded that the epidemiological correlation was so strong that alcohol simply must be carcinogenic! However, before the reformed alcoholic contemplates switching to water, he must weigh up other research, reported in the *Daily Telegraph*, which found that soft water is associated with heart disease and some other waters with Alzheimer's.

Those who think that sport and exercise provide a corrective to unhealthy eating and drinking, should also beware. They will know to avoid boxing as what *The Times* described as THE NOBLE ART OF BRAIN DAMAGE, though it has caused many fewer deaths than medical negligence. But what of the more popular cults of jogging and the gym? *The Times* reported that 'men who over-exercise have lower hormone levels' and warned that joggers are at increased risk from 'post-disease viral fatigue syndrome'. It was the *Daily Telegraph* which found space for the headline: FATAL SLIP OF MAN EXHAUSTED ON RUNNING MACHINE over a report on a fit 46-year-old tool-maker who died after collapsing from fatigue and hitting his head on a health machine. Since thousands of people apparently use treadmill machines, the *Telegraph* hastened to assure readers: 'Health & safety officials are to investigate.' They will have their work cut out since the Consumer Association in 1997 announced GOING TO THE GYM CAN BE BAD FOR YOUR HEALTH. Nor is the danger confined to a few fitness freaks. The *Sunday Times* recently uncovered five million fitness fanatics in Britain and reported an estimate that they cost the NHS £170 million a year in treatment for injuries, such as sprains, torn muscles and damaged cartilage, as well as treatment for exhaustion – without contributing to the high taxes on smokers who, remember pay for almost a quarter of the NHS!

Anyone seeking safety by staying at home should be alerted to the incidence of fatal domestic accidents, and if thinking of acquiring a budgerigar for company might ponder the headline PET BIRDS BLAMED FOR LUNG CANCER in the *Independent*, which reported that people who have kept birds are seven times more likely to get lung cancer. There's no space here to recall the hysterical warnings of an Aids epidemic, but a collector's piece from WHO, again, on World Aids Day was the solemn recommendation that 'kissing on the cheek' was safer than 'heavy sensual, so-called, French kissing'.

One of the most alarming health headlines of 1997 appeared surprisingly in the Money section of the *Sunday Times*: CANCER GASES THREATEN HOUSE PRICES. The story reported that 'millions of properties ... could see their values plummet' because of underground gases that cause cancer and explosions. The trouble appears to be

the seepage of methane gas from old landfill sites and the release of radon ... rated as the second-highest cause of lung cancer in Britain.

In May 1998, *The Times* thundered: RADON BLAMED FOR 1 IN

20 LUNG CANCER DEATHS, over a story from the *British Journal of Cancer* that about 1,800 people die each year in England from breathing radioactive gas. Perhaps inevitably, the researchers threw in that 'the problem was exacerbated by smoking' but (mysteriously) that smoking 'did not affect the overall proportion of those who became ill'.

If readers find difficulty coming to terms with all these warnings, I suspect they'd rather not know that the European Parliament has voted £38 million for a research study of:

> all possible mobile phone dangers, from brain cancer and leukaemia through to the effects on sleep patterns ...

No doubt, journalists are sometimes responsible for exaggerated or conflicting health stories. Thus in February 1998, the medical editor of the *Daily Telegraph* reported:

> The rates of cancer are not falling as fast as they should. People were continuing to smoke and young people were replacing those who died.

Four days later, the medical correspondent of *The Times* rejoiced:

> Over a 30-year period, the incidence of lung cancer fell annually by 2 or 3% more than was expected from the fall in tobacco consumption.

Up, down? Yes, no? Good, bad? To be, or not to be ...? What should we make of it all?

Yes, everything!

Before the reader becomes exhausted, I will draw to a merciful close with a shrewd and perhaps consoling thought from the American wit, P.J. O'Rourke:

> Everything that's fun in life is dangerous. And everything that isn't fun is dangerous too. It's impossible to be alive and safe.

That serves succinctly to explain my rooted objection to all those gruesome health warnings in capital letters on cigarettes and tobacco – that SMOKING KILLS or CAN KILL or CAUSES HEART DISEASE or DAMAGES THE HEALTH OF THOSE AROUND YOU. It's not merely that they are – as we shall see – either completely untrue, grossly exaggerated, or meaningless weasel phrases, but that by singling out smoking as uniquely dangerous, they lower our guard against other unsuspected dangers. If the old caution of *caveat emptor* has lost its force, perhaps we should fall back with the columnist, Ferdinand Mount, on his universal warning: 'Living can harm your health.'

Part I

The battleground

1

The follies and the crimes

'History', said Gibbon, 'is, indeed, little more than the register of the crimes, follies, and misfortunes of mankind.' In the history of smoking, the follies are perhaps rather more prominent than the crimes, but the latter are certainly not lacking.

One thing we know for certain is that when Columbus landed in the New World he was met by people who gave him some dried leaves in token of friendship. This was on the island he named San Salvador, which is thought to be that now known as Watling Island, though he thought it was Asia. This was on Friday 12 October 1492. Later, on 5 November, two of his crew met people who carried burning fire-brands with which to kindle some dry leaves, they said, in order to scent themselves. This began a process of misunderstanding about smoking tobacco which has continued to this day.

The usual arguments between experts began. Who had first brought tobacco to Europe? What actual tobacco plant was it? Was that which was first seen in fact a herb called perebecenuc? What are the origins of the word tobacco? It is perhaps worth mentioning that of two of the men who disputed the matter, Jean Nicot (who gave his name to nicotine) and Brother Andre Thevet, that the first lived to be 70, a good age in those days, and the second to 90, a good age at any time.

What was certain was that tobacco was at first hailed as a valuable remedy against all sorts of illnesses. Catherine de Medici used it, in the form of snuff, as a remedy for her headaches, starting a French habit of snuff-taking that endured for centuries. Later, one Dr Johannes Vittich claimed:

There can be no doubt that tobacco can cleanse all impurities and disperse every gross and viscous humour, as we find by daily experience. It cures cancer of the breast, open and eating sores, scabs and scratches, however poisonous and septic, goitre, broken limbs, erysipelas, and many other things. It will heal wounds in the arms, legs and other members of the body, of however long standing.'

It was also supposed to prevent the bubonic plague, and in 1636, in an outbreak in Nijmegen in the Netherlands, Dr Isbrand van Diemerbroek, who remained to help the sufferers when others had fled, said that he survived because he smoked. Once, when he thought that he would surely go under, he hurried home and smoked six or seven pipes of tobacco, and was sure this had saved his life.

In London Samuel Pepys recorded in his famous diary that he had seen two or three houses marked with a red cross on the doors, 'which was a sad sight to me'. So he had to buy some roll-tobacco to smell and to chew, which took away the apprehension.

There have been many other tributes paid to tobacco, from all over the world. The Hottentots used it against scorpion bites. The Chinese used it to treat colds and skin diseases, as well as malaria, skin parasites and obesity. The boys of Eton College were told to smoke a pipe a day to keep them healthy, and were beaten if they did not.

But the claims made were clearly unrealistic, and soon there was a reaction. It was obvious that tobacco could not cure broken bones or syphilis (which was also claimed for it). True to Martin Luther's observation that the human race is like a man falling off a donkey, first on the right side and then on the left, the revulsion was as violent as the devotion had been.

The 'expert' king

And it was led by a king, even though this was only King James I of England and VI of Scotland, surely one of the most unattractive figures ever to sit on a throne. Henri IV of France, who was one of the most attractive, called him 'the wisest fool in Christendom', thereby perhaps designating him the first known 'expert'.

James's attack on smoking is worth analysing in some detail because it is basically the same as that still endlessly used today. He starts off by saying that kings are useful as 'monitors' (perhaps today we would read 'nannies'), thereby it seems staking his claim to be an expert like those who continue to plague us today. He goes on to say that tobacco is a common herb, first found by the barbarous Indians, as he calls them, and used by them to cure the pox (syphilis), which they often suffer from because of their dirty habits. James was not known for any particular affection for soap and water himself.

As the Indians first brought that most detestable disease into Christendom (this was a common belief at the time and for long after), so they also introduced tobacco, as a 'stinking and unsavoury antidote'. 'The stinking Suffumigation' he goes on excitedly, 'whereof they yet use against that disease, making so one canker or venom to eat out another.'

The king seems to have been not only one of the first anti-smokers but also a prominent racist: 'barbarous and beastly manners' ... 'the wild, godless and slavish Indians' ... 'so vile and stinking a custom' ... 'the vile barbarous custom'; we can see where some of the modern anti-smokers got their ideas on the right way to state their case.

Then we have the first hint of 'addiction', that other favourite modern term of abuse, itself with malicious undertones of helpless weak-willed characters caught in foul toils, though, as the late great psychologist Professor Eysenck, who has been called the most quoted intellectual in the world after Freud and Marx, has said:

[Smoking] is not an addiction because the term 'addiction' really has no scientific meaning; it is used in so many different ways that it is almost impossible to attach any meaning to it. This idea is not really controversial; there have been several books on it recently with people making exactly the same point. You could call sex addictive, or reading in my case, or playing tennis; you can call anything addictive which a person does routinely and which he would be sorry to stop doing and which might have all sorts of repercussions on his mental and physical life.

King James did not use the word 'addiction', because it doesn't seem to have been invented then, but he says:

... many in this kingdom have had such a continual use of taking this unsavoury smoke, as now they are not able to forbear the same, no more than an old drunkard can abide to be long sober ....

There is more unpleasant language: 'this vile custom' ... 'the filthy abuse thereof'. 'Filthy' seems to have survived into modern times as a favourite term, so we often have to bear the words 'filthy habit' being spat at us. King James himself was known to drink in a way that struck even that hard-drinking age.

'Are you not guilty of sinful and shameful lust?' On the whole no, if the usual meaning is given to that term. But of course any nasty word will do. Professor Glantz, a leading American anti-smoker, was responsible for the possibly seminal statement at a conference in Australia in 1990:

> The main thing the science has done [on the issue of environmental tobacco smoke, or 'passive smoking'] in addition to help people like me to pay mortgages, is it has legitimized the concerns that people have that they don't like cigarette smoke. And that is a strong emotional force that needs to be harnessed and used. We're on a roll, and the bastards are on the run.

Presumably he has no reason to believe that smokers are more likely than others to have been born out of wedlock, but 'bastard' is an ugly, hurtful word, well suited to his purpose. To return to King James:

> And for the vanities committed in this filthy custom, is it not both great vanity and uncleanness, that at the table, a place of respect, of cleanliness, of modesty, men should not be ashamed to sit tossing of Tobacco pipes, and Puffing of the smoke of Tobacco one to another, making the filthy smoke and stink thereof ....

Since we know of James that he didn't wash his hands ('I kiss your dirty hands' wrote one of his favourites), and dribbled, he could have been no very pleasant table companion himself.

He was justified in making fun of the claims that tobacco cured disease (though it is now known that smokers do have a lower rate of some diseases, notably Parkinson's, Alzheimer's, and cancer of the womb), but he immediately went on to what sound like very modern claims. Tobacco caused all sorts of diseases, including filling the lungs with soot, again a curiously modern false claim, and was 'harmful to the brain'; though we now know that it stimulates the brain; 'dangerous to the lungs'; and 'hateful to the nose', bringing thoughts of all those excitable people who declare that the mere smell of a cigarette will do the most dreadful things to them, including one on the Internet who said that it causes her to drop dead in exactly one minute.

So you think you're free?

But what was far more sinister, if it had only been realised, was an earlier passage, which is worth the effort of decoding:

> … is it not the greatest sin of all, that you the people of all sorts of this Kingdom, who are created and ordained by God to bestow both your persons and goods for the maintenance both of the honour and safety of your King and Commonwealth, should disable yourselves in both? He cannot be thought able for any service in the wars that cannot endure oftentimes the want of meat, drink, and sleep, much more then must he endure the want of Tobacco. But now if it were time of wars, and that you were to make some sudden Cavalcado upon your enemies, if any of you should seek leisure to stay behind his fellow for taking of Tobacco, for my part I should be sorry [*sic*] for any evil chance that might befall him.

The meaning is not quite clear: does he mean that his comrades would see to it that an evil chance would befall him because he wasn't with them in the attack, or that the enemy would be able to catch him, or what? As James himself had no experience of fighting, and was indeed a famed coward, he probably had no very clear idea himself of what he wanted to say. He could have pointed out that the Englishmen of his predecessor's reign were certainly not famed for being behindhand in any Cavalcado, though smoking was common amongst them.

But this is sinister in that the King is putting forward the National Socialist (and Marxist Socialist) theory that the citizen exists for the good of the state, indeed that his body more or less belongs to the state. Even modern anti-smokers would presumably pay lip-service to the democratic idea that prefers to see the state as existing for the good of the citizen, however much the state itself tries to disabuse us of it. The more a state wants to extend its powers, the more it is likely to put forward this idea in one form or another. We now see it happening in this country, in that much of the propaganda about 'the nation's health' implies that it's your duty to see that you are in good health. You must eat whatever it is that the latest experts have declared is good for you, and take exercise, and drink bottled water, and not smoke, and the rest of it, so that you are not a drain on the resources of the state.

It has been pointed out that if you do indeed do all these things that are good for you, and are, perhaps, rewarded by a very long life, you are likely to be much more of a drain on the state by requiring nursing through the endless horrible years of Alzheimer's and the other terrible rewards of the dutiful citizen. Hitler solved this problem by suggesting that good Germans should commit suicide when they reached the age of 60, though as he approached that age himself I don't think he raised the matter again.

To return to King James, why did he feel as he did? It has been suggested that it was his personal hatred of that much greater man and far more attractive personality, Sir Walter Raleigh, who if he did not actually introduce tobacco into England did much to make it popular, that lay behind his passion. In his polemic he actually mentions 'a custom brought in by a father so generally hated.' There seems to be no evidence that Raleigh was 'so generally hated', but certainly James himself was far from popular, what with his personal habits, his favourites, the scandals about his unsavoury court, his attempts at appeasement of the great enemy Spain, and his quarrels with his parliaments. It may be that it was jealousy of one man, a mean hatred, that moved him.

It is somehow pleasant to know that Raleigh smoked a pipe before his execution, and on the scaffold ran his fingers along the axe, saying it was 'a sure cure for all ills'. And then called on the executioner, who hesitated (which is also nice to know), saying: 'Strike, man, strike!' Perhaps the executioner too was a smoker.

But there's money in it

So James went on, like later anti-smokers, to ponder how he could make money out of this hatred of his. He did it very simply, by placing a huge tax on tobacco. The smokers retaliated, naturally, by taking to smuggling on an enormous scale. Eventually, with the rise in importance of the export of tobacco from the colony of Virginia, James took the trade into his own hands and created a royal monopoly. So much for his real feelings about the filthy 'stinking Suffumigation'.

James was so determined to keep the profits in his own hands that he carried on a fierce struggle against the growers of tobacco in England. This was solely because they were cutting into his profits on the trade. The battle went on till the end of the century, but finally the interests of the colony and the king's pocket prevailed, and tobacco growing here ceased.

Sir William Paddy, King James's physician, was a great smoker himself, and lived to be 80. James himself made a mere 58.

The English went on smoking, and in the Civil War both sides smoked equally. Smoking was spreading all over Europe. It had come to the East even earlier. The Japanese were introduced to it by traders in a Portuguese ship blown off course in 1542, and by the end of the century the Emperor was growing tobacco in his own gardens. The Japanese term for 'tobacco merchant' was first recorded in 1578. A particularly dictatorial Shogun or Prime Minister (who represented the real power in the country) tried to stop it in 1609, with severe penalties for smokers and tobacco sellers. This does not seem to have been for health reasons; more perhaps for that oldest of motives, sheer love of exercising power. Whatever his motives, the attempt failed, and sixteen years later the Japanese were smoking as before.

Smoking also spread in China, and again an attempt was made to stop it, this time by the last Emperor of the Ming dynasty, which was conquered three years later by the Manchus, who were smokers themselves. It was brought to Africa, again by the Portuguese and later by the Dutch. Settlers found it a profitable crop, and soon started a good trade with the Hottentots.

It spread too in India, though the high-caste Brahmins were against it because it might lead to ritual impurity, since to carry anything to the lips more than once could lead to it being contaminated with a bodily excrement. It is probably best not to ask how they thought this could happen. Members of the lower castes and other faiths had no such inhibitions, and smoked readily. Snuff too was used by all, even the Brahmins. It was from India that we got the cigar, the word once used for it, 'cheroot', being a corruption of a Tamil word.

An exemplary anti-smoker

Smoking spread too in the great Turkish Empire, which at one time looked as if it might conquer Europe in the West as well as much of the East, together with the Middle East and North Africa. It was as well for smokers in Europe that it didn't, because in 1632 there came to power that Sultan who might be seen as the patron saint of the anti-smokers, Murad IV. (He had officially started his reign in 1623, as a boy of nine.) Abusing smokers and taking taxes from them were not enough for him. He killed them.

Before him other Sultans had punished smokers by having their pipes thrust through their noses and parading them through the streets in this condition. This was not enough for Murad. He had them beheaded on the spot, and left their bodies in the streets for an example. Even in his wars he would make a point of seeking out smokers among his own men and killing them by hanging, beheading, cutting them into quarters, or crushing their hands and feet and leaving them to perish on the field. There is a story that when he caught one of his gardeners and his wife smoking, he had their legs amputated and exhibited them as they bled to death.

When he at last died, at the age of 28, from the effects of drink, he had killed well over 100,000 of his own people, many with his own hand. Drinking alcohol is, of course, forbidden to Moslems. Tobacco is not. The Koran was written long before it was introduced. Perhaps Murad's hatred of smoking came from the well-known Puritan tendency to:

> Compound for sins they feel inclined to
> By damning those they have no mind to.

In this respect there may well be plenty of other Murads among us today.

No other anti-smoker has soared to Murad's heights in persecution, but throughout most of his century sporadic efforts at violence were made. In parts of the Holy Roman Empire smoking could carry the death penalty.

In Russia smokers were flogged, had their lips slit, were exiled to Siberia, or, in a curious attempt to cure the habit, castrated. In Switzerland, with something of the same sort of reasoning, it seems, smoking was included in the commandment against adultery. Offenders could be beaten with rods, branded, or exiled.

Even in the American colonies, where so much of their hard-won prosperity was based on the tobacco trade, and the economic future of Virginia and Maryland depended on tobacco, there were persecutions of smokers. In Connecticut in 1650 it was decreed that no one under 21 should be allowed to smoke, 'nor any other that hath not already accustomed himself to the use thereof'. And even then he had to get a doctor's certificate that smoking would be 'useful for him, and also that he hath received a licence from the Court for the same' (this is interesting, because it suggests that the ban was not for health reasons). After all that, he could not smoke 'in the streets, highways, or any barnyards, or upon training days in any open places, under the penalty of sixpence for each offence'.

Smoking was forbidden on the Sabbath all over New England within two miles of the meeting house. In fact, about the only place the smoker could have his pipe in peace was in his own home, and in many parts of the US that state of affairs has returned. It only remains for the modern 'Land of the Free' to bring back the scarlet letter worn on the breast of the sinner: not A for adulterer but S for smoker.

None of this, however, stopped the good folk of Connecticut from starting to go into the business of growing and selling tobacco themselves.

Before this an unpleasant new development took place in France. In 1629 Cardinal Richelieu, who disliked smoking as much as he liked conquest and power, imposed a tax on tobacco with the excuse that if it were too cheap it would hurt the health of the people. We're taxing you, that is, because it's *good* for you. Aren't we nice?

It has been suggested that there must have been strong reasons for such violent persecution. There aren't any that can be clearly defined, apart from the natural human desire to stop other people

enjoying themselves. What better way to demonstrate your power?
And if you can also make money from it, what more can you ask?

The spirit of William Tell

Switzerland, apart from equating smoking and adultery, in 1675
set up a small Inquisition-type organisation, known as the Tobacco
Chamber, to deal with offenders. But the Swiss resisted, and the
Tobacco Chamber, after the first few years, grew moribund. In
1706 smoking was declared to be not absolutely forbidden, but as
a rearguard action it was decreed that no one was to smoke where
there was a danger of fire, on pain of a fine.

Three years later the prohibition of tobacco was repealed because it was not possible to enforce it. Then a heavy tax was levied
on all smokers and snuff-takers. Again the people's resistance was
so determined that a month later it was taken off.

Sometimes we fail to appreciate what a contribution the little
state of Switzerland has made to human freedom.

In Russia the punishments were dropped when Peter the Great
took to smoking. The Church authorities had declared that anyone
who smoked would be excommunicated, as would anyone be who
was clean-shaven. Then Peter came back from a trip to Europe
smoking and went round with a pair of scissors cutting off any
beards that came his way. As usual, he got what he wanted, and
peace came to the smokers of Russia.

So in spite of all the taxes, punishments and abuse, people went
on smoking. Even *Le Roi Soleil*, Louis XIV, with all his absolutism,
could not stop his own daughters smoking. They borrowed their
pipes from the Swiss Guard.

In the eighteenth century, the years of the 'Enlightenment', little
attempt was made to stop smoking. It was always pipes that were
smoked, except in Spain and the many countries under Spanish
rule or influence, where cigars were usual. Agricultural labourers
in England used to smoke pipes made of walnut shells, with straws
for stems. They sound charming, but we are not told how they
prevented them burning up. The rich, women as well as men,
smoked silver pipes, but the usual pipe, for all classes and both
sexes, was clay.

Then snuff became the rage.

Smutchin and sneeshin-mills

As we have seen, when tobacco was first introduced in the sixteenth century, snuff was used as medicine. It soon became more than that, and by the following century one James Howell, imprisoned by the Commonwealth for something or other, probably for enjoying himself, wrote entertaining letters in which he described how the Spaniards and the Irish took snuff, 'and it mightily refreshes the brain'. In Ireland, he said, 'the serving maid upon the washing-block, and the swain upon the ploughshare when they are tir'd with labour, take out their boxes of *smutchin* and draw it into their nostrils with a quill, and it will beget new spirits in them with a fresh vigour to fall to their work again ....'

Snuff soon reached the Highlands, and became so much of a recognised local custom that later the wooden figure of a Highlander with his snuff mull or grinder was the sign of a tobacco shop. Sometimes this grinder was called a *sneeshin-mill*.

It is sometimes said that the courtiers of Charles II brought back the habit of taking snuff when they returned from their exile in France, but since Howell speaks of it as an established habit in Ireland when he was there in 1639, it is more likely that it was already established in England too, but among the 'serving maid upon the washing block and the swain upon the ploughshare' rather than in fashionable circles. Wherever it came from, it quickly became high fashion. It was easier to carry about a little box rather than a pipe and some kindling, which before the invention of matches would have been in the form of a flint and steel, with charred linen as tinder.

Snuff boxes too could be little works of art, and collecting them started early. But the custom had a tremendous boost when Admiral Sir George Rooke, in an attack remarkable for courage and cheek, captured a Spanish fleet escorting a French convoy carrying many thousand barrels of snuff. This, as it happens, was very useful in two ways: as a valuable 'prize', and then when Sir George's ship was in great danger after one of the merchantmen loaded with snuff was set on fire and blew up, 'the snuff, in some measure, extinguished the fire, and preserved the English man-of-war from being consumed'. Fifty tons of the best Havana snuff were distributed to the officers and

crew as prize money, and it was sold for fourpence a pound in all
the south coast ports.

In England pipe-smoking remained popular for agricultural
labourers and the like, but snuff-taking was gaining ground every
day. There were not lacking, of course, people who said that it was
unfeminine and women shouldn't do it, but women paid no attention, and there were many highly scented varieties on the market.
We hear of snuff scented with attar of roses and ambergris, mint
and rose leaves, bitter almonds and cloves.

Because of the danger of fire on wooden ships, snuff soon began
to replace the pipe in the Royal Navy and the merchant fleet, and
even the quid of chewing tobacco that had become traditional.
Since there is not much to be said for chewing tobacco, or quid-
ding, since it inevitably leads to spitting, this was no doubt a step
forward. It remained very common, however, in the American
colonies and later United States, and the horror expressed by
European travellers such as Thackeray and Dickens at the universal habit does something to explain the continuing protest by some
American citizens.

For the protests never quite died away, even when snuffing and
smoking were almost universal habits. Smoking a pipe, for instance, was inelegant in the presence of ladies, we learn from *The
Diverting History of John Gilpin*, written in 1785, though there was
certainly no such rule about snuff. Fanny Burney, in attendance at
about the same date on the very correct and respectable Queen of
George III, was entrusted with the task of mixing the Queen's
snuff.

'No lady'

It is difficult to ascertain why smoking suddenly became unrespect-
able and unladylike (dread phrase) in the nineteenth century. Men
of all classes continued to smoke, though snuff went out of fashion
among all but old men and old working-class women (who also
smoked when they could get tobacco). It has been suggested that it
was with the introduction of briar and meerschaum pipes that this
swift change of mood came about. A dainty little clay pipe was one
thing, a hefty briar or meerschaum another. In the scanty dresses
of the earliest part of the century it would not have been easy to

carry in a pocket, and 'reticules' were usually little bags of comparatively delicate material.

Or was it perhaps part of the general legend, industriously fostered by women of the middle classes especially, that women, 'ladies', were somehow of better and finer stuff than those base animals, men? 'Ladies' did not drink, except a glass of sherry and wine with dinner, they did not swear, they did not fight; nor did they indulge in another habit associated with men, that is smoking. It was one of the things that marked the 'lady'.

'Women' did smoke, though, especially naughty ones. Georges Sand shocked even the comparatively easy French society at the beginning of the century by smoking cigars, though she added to the shock by having numerous lovers and writing sexy novels. Still, the way in which the cigars were picked on suggests that this habit was regarded as almost as shocking as the others.

Smoking, then, became something that working women and prostitutes did. This in itself was a subtle attack on smoking. Again in France, always supposed to be more tolerant than Anglo-Saxon countries, we find two almost contemporaneous attacks, from opposite ends of the political spectrum. In 1867 the reactionary Catholic writer Louis François Veuillot speaks with horror of having been to a café where not only women, but *ladies* smoked. The revolutionary newspaper *Le Combat* attacked the women of Paris who had emasculated and depraved the young by drinking beer and smoking. This sort of thing finds its parallel in modern claims by the anti-smokers that they have made smoking socially unacceptable, and the smoker an outcast; they are very proud of this.

Even in the nineteenth century, however, some 'ladies' continued to smoke, though usually they were those whose social position was so unassailable that they could get away with anything. It was difficult to say that the daughter of the Czar of Russia and daughter-in-law of the Queen-Empress Victoria, Marie, Duchess of Edinburgh, was low or immoral – at least to her face – or the Empress Eugènie of France, though both shocked others by smoking in public. Later in the century it became a sign of the 'new woman', educated, independent, and often regarded as slightly outrageous.

It became very much simpler for women (and ladies) to smoke when cigarettes were introduced, because they were much easier to handle than pipes or cigars. They had been regularly smoked in Spain, Portugal, Italy, Russia and France, but did not make their way to Britain until after the Crimean War. The first factory in Britain was set up in the 1850s at Walworth by a Scot, Robert Peacock Gloag, formerly paymaster to the Turkish forces in the Crimea. Being easier to handle than pipes, and cheaper than cigars, cigarettes soon became very popular. (In 1888 *Wild Woodbine* were five for a penny, while a loaf of best bread cost sixpence.)

Apart from the comparatively mild attack on women smokers, smokers were left alone in most places except in the home of tobacco and land of the free. The anti movement rumbled on, often hand in hand with that against drink. Children would go colour-blind if they smoked. They would go bald, be stunted, go insane, be sterile, impotent, and sexually promiscuous, all at once. The feeling was so strong in some parts that, for instance, when a touring opera staged *Carmen* in Kansas in the 1890s, the location of the first act was changed from the front of a tobacco factory to that of a dairy. Perhaps the march of the toreadors was changed to the parade of the milkfloats. And every time the libretto required the heroine to light a cigarette, did she drink a glass of milk?

What saved the smokers this time was the utter failure of prohibition in the 1920s and 1930s. When prohibition was brought in, the celebrated preacher Billy Sunday said: 'Prohibition is won, now for tobacco.' But prohibition turned into a costly and disastrous failure, and even the most earnest puritans were discouraged.

A very important part was played, too, by the two world wars. Everyone smokes in war. 'Smoke 'em if you've got 'em' provides a little break in the beastliness. If you haven't got much, or anything at all, to eat, it eases the hunger pains. A cigarette is the first thing the casualty asks for. The cigarette offered is a sign of comradeship. For the prisoner of war, it shows that he has fallen into the hands of civilised captors. In air-raids, the little rituals and politenesses involved in the sharing of cigarettes break the tension.

Better than Murad

But even in the second world war anti-smoker forces were gathering, led by no less a champion than Adolf Hitler. Some of his ideas were curiously 'state-of-the-art' by modern standards. He was a vegetarian, very keen on nature and animals and what we now call ecology, very anti-religious (though he kept this under wraps to some extent for political reasons). He talked incessantly of the People (*das Volk*), and Youth, and the glorious new future. He was also extremely anti-smoking; why, no one seems to know. Like anti-Semitism, it was an idea that was about in Germany as in other parts of the world. In 1934, for instance, an otherwise unknown Herr Bonne is on record as having said that alcohol, nicotine, and syphilis were the three causes of degeneracy in German youth. The remedy he suggested was sterilisation. Wherever it came from, Hitler's anti-smokerism was very real. He refused to let anyone smoke in his presence, and in 1942 he gave 100,000 marks of his own money to the first 'Institute for the Struggle against Tobacco'. In *Hitler's Table Talk* (OUP, 1988) this remark of his is quoted: 'I have no notice on my door, but smokers aren't admitted.'

It isn't surprising that German scientists discovered evidence of the dangers of smoking. What may surprise some is that in a programme on Channel Four in February 1998, this research was described approvingly. What was actually said at the beginning of the programme was that, in the institute where this research was carried on:

> a lot of the Reich's anti-tobacco work was performed. One can imagine these leaders of Nazi academia sitting around and at one sitting deciding the fate of Jews, at another deciding the fate of tobacco in Germany.

It was not actually mentioned that this same Nazi academia had supplied research showing that the Jews were inferior, and deserved to be exterminated. If, of course, you find it tolerable that the fate of the Jews and of tobacco should be spoken of in the same breath, and without other comment, there is nothing more to be said.

And in America recently a man condemned to death was refused the traditional last cigarette. Presumably they thought it would be bad for him.

'A boy from the next village'

Experts have defined the rules for the most disastrous and disgusting events of this century. Experts told us that some races were better than others, and some didn't deserve to live at all. Experts told us that all social problems could be solved if whole classes of people, with their families and all associated with them, were massacred, as in the old Soviet Union and elsewhere. On a lesser scale experts in education formulated progressive ideas that have resulted in horrifying large numbers of children leaving school almost unable to read or write. Other experts told us to put up the tower blocks that are now a major social problem.

Yet most of these experts are self-defined. They tell us they're experts; they have qualifications on paper (and we seldom bother to try to find out whether these in fact have anything to do with the subject they're being expert about), and they write articles or books at some length, mostly in a jargon that few of us can begin to understand.

A cynical East European defined an expert as 'a boy from the next village' – that is, someone we don't know. We don't know how honest he is, or whether he is an idiot, or what has been called a 'clever-silly'. This is close to James I as the 'wisest fool'. We should surely be warned by a fact that more and more of us are beginning to notice: that when you get experts called in to decide on some knotty point, they disagree. And we never hear of them losing credibility because of this, or their jobs, or their clients. Presumably they all just go on being experts.

This sort of disagreement, of course, is as old as human history. One of the first things that a student of Ancient Egypt observes is that if there is only one piece of evidence about an event, this is taken for gospel. If there are two, it is equally taken for gospel that they will flatly contradict each other. Pharaoh Ramses II covered the walls of temples with pictures and inscriptions about his great victory in the battle of Kadesh against the Hittites. When the Hittites' account of the battle was discovered, it seemed that they had won.

The great Greek historian, Herodotus, was one of the few who recognised this human trait. His history, written in the fifth century BC, should be a model for all historians, in that he often gives conflicting stories about events, and leaves us to make up our own minds.

When two opposing views are offered, it is often pure chance that decides which version shall be accepted. The Greek historian Plutarch gave a version of the story of Antony and Cleopatra that happened to be turned into a masterpiece by Shakespeare; his contemporary the Jewish Josephus, possibly the better historian, and nearer to the world of high politics than Plutarch, describes Cleopatra as a monster of greed and ambition, and so unattractive that she couldn't even seduce the susceptible Herod, whose reaction was to consider murdering her. Josephus also writes that Antony was a pederast. We accept Plutarch's version because of Shakespeare.

We can all think of other examples of experts in collision, but unfortunately nowadays there is a tiresome new development: experts disagree as much as ever they did, but they tend not to do so simultaneously so that we can compare their views as they appear. Now they seem to do it serially. That is, all available experts will agree that, for example, meat and milk and eggs are very good for you. So we all eat them. Then they will all simultaneously change their minds, and say they are very bad for you.

Do we all then give up these everyday foods? Many of us do, but others have learnt that it is best to continue eating them peacefully, and wait for the next change in expert opinion. Young people are at a disadvantage in this, because they can't remember what the experts said last time.

There is no doubt that many of the experts are very well-meaning indeed. Most of us are familiar with the sort of person who has a fixed idea about, say, aliens and the Pyramids. He has no other subject of conversation, and can talk about it for hours. The truth has been revealed to him, and he wants, very kindly as he sees it, to share it with us. Such people are often quite normal in other ways, and harmless. They only become harmful when they have the qualifications and the wish to set themselves up as expert scientists. Monomaniac scientists are dangerous, even if they do keep away from ideas such as the massacre of the inferior race or the class enemy.

It is perhaps not so much that their ideas are dangerous in themselves, but that they insist that they are the only ones. Just as the 'aliens in the Pyramids' enthusiast insists that it is the most important thing that has ever happened in human history, and that all our lives will change as a result, so the medical enthusiast declares that all human ills are caused by whatever the present experts have declared to be what causes all human ills, and nothing else matters.

The Victorians laid great stress upon diet. 'You are what you eat' was a catchphrase. 'I am convinced digestion is the great secret of life' wrote the famous wit Sydney Smith in 1837. Then disease came to be supposed to be caused mostly by heredity, or 'bad blood on *your* side of the family', as it was often put. Round about the beginning of the twentieth century 'germs' came to the public attention, and every disease was regarded as the result of infection.

Later, in this century, we discovered Freud, and all ills became psychological, and your mother's fault. For the Americans, of course, it was drink, and prohibition was to solve all their problems. Now it is smoking, but there are signs that it is shifting back to heredity again, with our genes blamed for everything from homosexuality to bad temper.

Diet too is coming back, with a steady attack mounted on sugar some time ago; also salt, butter, and of course eggs and meat, soft drinks and coffee. Interestingly, the Victorians decided that it was tea that was the enemy of the human race, and said nothing about coffee. You could put together a fascinating list of all the foods and drinks that have been declared by experts at one time or another to be bad for you, and you would probably end up living on porridge and water. And the water would have be in bottles, and very expensive.

Surely no one with any sense would deny that diet is very important. Just look into people's trolleys in supermarkets, and then look at the people pushing them: the fragile young couple with fragile children in tow and a trolley full of frozen fast food and synthetic soft drinks; the sad fat lady with the trolley full of dough-nuts.

Certainly there are still many dangerous and unpleasant infec-tions about, and some that were thought to have been eradicated are making a comeback. These infections damage our immune systems, and make us more likely to contract other diseases. There's no doubt too that heredity plays a considerable part in our physical well-being or lack of it. There are specific problems asso-ciated with drugs, alcohol, and tobacco abuse.

Above all, there is the curious modern tendency to a complete separation of body and mind, so that the assumption seems to be that they co-exist without any interaction: a man or woman with every kind of real or imaginary worry about the present and future is to be treated exactly the same as some cheerful extrovert with nothing particular to worry about except the disease of the mo-ment. This seems so obviously silly that it is rather troubling to find that there are experts who still maintain it, or something like it. Surely we should accept that all these factors play a part in health, and that concentrating on one and dismissing all the others is not in the least helpful. Yet that is exactly what many experts do.

Two thousand years of TB

A very good example of what experts can do is shown in the history of tuberculosis. In 1908 the British government agreed that it was a highly infectious disease, caused by Koch's bacillus, and that sections of the laws applying to the prevention of infectious disease should apply to TB. This was hailed a a great modern scientific advance. Yet the medical writings attributed to Hippocrates (of the Hippocratic oath), put together in the fourth century BC, had listed TB among the epidemics. The theory of contagion ('catching') had been plainly set out by Hyeronymous Fracastorius in 1546. In England in 1689 Richard Morton listed nine causes of the disease, some obvious enough, such as the physical condition, bad air, and youth, which certainly play their part, but his ninth cause was simply 'contagion'.

From 1699 onwards governments acted upon this knowledge. The Italian Republic of Lucca was the first. Spain and other southern states followed. Strict laws were passed to guard the populace from infection. But France declared against the theory, and her influence at that time was enormous. All through the two following centuries, in most parts of the world, highly infectious patients mingled with their families and friends, and millions died. Various causes were suggested, but most popular was indulging in 'the passions'. You shouldn't feel so strongly about anything that it affected your health. Keats' 'passion' for Fanny Brawne was considered to be one of the causes of his death, the other being his feelings about the cruel reviews of his works. It was nothing to do with the fact that he had spent a long time nursing his brother who was dying of TB.

But by the end of the century 'heredity' was considered the most likely cause, and this notion lasted, at least in the popular view, well into this century, in spite of the clear evidence from Koch and others. It meant that the parents could be blamed, since with their bad heredity they shouldn't have married and had children at all.

Then at last the infectious nature of the disease was recognised here. It was not a particularly striking triumph for science, in that it had taken well over two thousand years for the truth to be rediscovered.

But we are cleverer than our ancestors, and it can't happen nowadays, can it? Certainly we know more than our ancestors, because we know what they found out. But whether we are putting this knowledge to any better use is another matter.

Cancer has been known from the earliest times. Egyptian mummies show signs of it. It was no very great problem when most people died before they were forty, since it is a disease mostly of the old. But we find it mentioned as contagious in the account of a clinic set up in France in the seventeenth century. In 1762 Richard Guy in England wrote that 'the cancerous humour is a Virus ....' In 1842 William Budd of the British Medical Society noted the link between cancer of the penis in men and cervical or uterine cancer in their wives. Hospitals set aside special wards for cancer patients, and in New York a special hospital was built for them. In 1902 the entry on cancer in the great German encyclopaedia, *Brockhaus*, declared that it was not yet certain whether the cause was heredity or contagion. Six years later it seemed that the question had been answered.

In 1908 Ellerman and Bang in Denmark identified a virus causing leukaemia in chickens, and in 1910 Peyton Rous in America that causing chicken sarcoma (cancer). Similar work was done in Japan in 1911, and in the three following years Rous and Fujimani Inanoto found three more viruses in chickens and ducks. In 1917 Waelsch found the virus causing cancerous warts in human beings, and in 1919 Wile and Kinger in the US found the one causing human papillomata.

This considerable body of evidence, together with the knowledge from on-the-spot observation that had been accumulated in previous centuries, made it look as if the matter had been settled. Now, as with TB, it would be a matter of shielding patients from infecting others, and settling down to the question of finding appropriate drugs and treatments.

But this didn't happen. The viruses kept on turning up, and devoted investigators kept on finding them, but the experts blamed cancer on anything you like to mention except infection. Carcinogens (cancer-causing substances) were thought to include soot; bischloromethyl ether to which workers may be exposed in the chemical industry; vinyl chloride fumes in the rubber industry; asbestos; chrome; ionizing radiations; carcinogenic hydrocarbons produced by fires; urban pollution; hormonal secretions; natural foods such as peanuts and maize containing aflatoxins together with the Hepatitis B virus; man-made foods; the herb comfrey; mouldy bread and pickled vegetables; and a particular kind of salt-cured fish in China. Other cancer causing factors have been said to be: chewing betel nut in India; smoking cigars with the burning end in the mouth (this *is* done somewhere in the East); heredity; eating fat; being fat; being old; drinking alcohol and coffee; having an active sex life; having no sex life; and smoking. An article in the *Consumer Research Magazine*, May 1989, is headed:

Does everything cause cancer?

It looks as if it does. Keeping pet birds has been implicated. A recent list says that the birth-control pill greatly increases the risk of cervical and breast cancer; the injectable long-lasting contraceptive Depo-Provera is said to double the risk of breast cancer;

condoms, or the talc used on them, are linked with ovarian and breast cancer; as are in-vitro fertilisation and hormone replacement therapy. Men are more likely to develop prostate cancer if their mothers took hormones. X-rays can cause cancer; so, it is said, can fluoride in water; also living too close to electro-magnetic fields (EMFs), especially from power lines. But these can also be in your home: your VDU or oven, or even your vacuum cleaner, could be the enemy.

Many of the drugs prescribed for various conditions could be dangerous: cholesterol-lowering drugs, fertility drugs, diuretics, drugs for the lowering of blood pressure: all have been implicated, together with breast surgery, vasectomies, transplants, and Vitamin K given to new-born babies.

But where does the virus fit in? Very neatly: we all know that if we're 'run down' we're much more likely to get a cold or flu, or any other kind of infection that may be about. Certainly many of the modern drugs poured into us make us feel worse than the disease they were prescribed for. Indeed at any one time a considerable number of hospital beds are occupied by patients suffering from the effects of drug therapy.

Most of the 'causes' listed above represent some kind of unnatural strain put upon the body, which can be weakened by it. And then the virus pounces?

There is something else that should be taken seriously in the virus debate: by 1967 hamsters had been treated with an antitumour vaccine. Later cotton-top tamarin monkeys and cats were also immunised. Since 1975, *Black's Veterinary Dictionary* tells us, chickens have been routinely immunised against cancer.

Immunisation programmes for people have been carried out in Italy, Greece, and apparently in more than twenty other countries. And now we in this country are told that a vaccine is on the way. Let's hope it doesn't take another two thousand years. Meanwhile chickens and cats are being routinely immunised. Can this be because vets are unable to blame their patients' behaviour for their diseases? You can't tell a cat not to smoke, or a chicken not to give way to its passions.

The experts

When we assess the pronouncements of experts, we must bear in mind that it is risky to go against the mood of the age. Ralph Harris remarks that this is certainly the way of many economic gurus. With any luck the fashion will last long enough for you to make your name and perhaps even your pile, and if it does happen to change while you have not quite completed your work, you can switch to the new trend. There is always some human activity to be attacked. Global warming is a good recent example (a while ago, it was global freezing). If we were to take the warnings seriously and act upon them, it would mean a considerable impoverishment of the lifestyles not only of 'developed' nations, but also of those of nations that are earnestly trying to become developed. And it might turn out that the experts were quite wrong about global warming, and we were really in for a new ice age instead.

Yet there must be more to it than mere money-grubbing. The history of science is full of examples of eminent experts who have trifled with the truth for what often seems to be the desire for fame, or for acknowledgement, or to annoy their colleagues, or just, perhaps, for the fun of it. Although scientists have always been aware that members of their confraternity got up to this sort of thing, they have mostly preserved a decent silence about it. After all, as one doctor remarked, 'in the end they all have to work together'. But lately it has become so flagrant that counter-experts have been speaking out, and some reputations, of the dead as well as the living, have been shattered.

The still famous nineteenth-century German biologist Ernst Haeckel was widely admired for his remarkable drawings showing embryos of various creatures, including man, at various stages of development, proving that, true to the principles of evolution, they all appeared to pass through similar stages. This suited the dominant cult of evolution very nicely. However, it has now been shown that Haeckel faked his drawings. To take another example, the American physicist Robert Milligan won a Nobel prize in 1923 for work on the nature of the electron that ignored data with which he did not agree.

To what extent can fakers in the past have been influenced by then fashionable modes of thought? How much of what looks like dishonesty may simply have been the feeling that everyone knew that something couldn't or could be true, and who was the investigator to say that they were wrong and he was right?

This can't apply to someone like Haeckel, of course, who certainly knew what he was doing when he fabricated his beautiful and elaborate drawings; nor can it be said of modern scientists who deliberately fake or suppress data. But we know what the thought patterns are today, and so we are, or should be, better able to judge the skulduggery of the modern experts who cheat. Perhaps some of them are so conventionally-minded that they can't believe their own evidence if it conflicts with that of the current consensus. They should be pitied, but at the same time you shouldn't believe a word they say.

It is possible that some of them are sometimes right, but it is a waste of time to try to sort out such occasions from the others when they are certainly wrong. There are those who are merely incompetent, and muddle the facts because they don't know any better. Don't believe them either.

However, there can be no doubt about those who deliberately twist or concoct evidence, for money, or fame, or for any other reason. There is the well-known and widely respected consultant obstetrician who, in 1997, was proved beyond any doubt to have invented an account of the world's first example of the transplantation of an ectopic pregnancy, in which a fertilised egg grows outside the womb. Before that he had made up case-histories of more than 190 women supposed to have taken part in a trial of a hormone that prevented miscarriage. A consultant is certainly not short of money. This man was celebrated and admired in his own professional world. He was not going along with fashionable opinion: the transplantation of the ectopic pregnancy was seen as quite extraordinary. Did he want still more fame and admiration? Enough to risk absolute professional ruin if he was found out? We can never know, because even if he explained himself we couldn't believe him.

When evidence of this came up, medical journals were already worried about phoney claims based on doubtful research. One editor remarked on four cases having been found in one year. A professional 'Committee on Publications Ethics' has been set up to check on fraudulent research of this kind. No doubt it will do good work, but it is to be hoped that it will check its own members very carefully.

Damn the experiment

One motive suggested for this sort of faking is that in practice it is very difficult to make experiments go the way you think they should. Students know this; they also know that the right answer is printed at the back of the textbook, so it is not difficult to fix it so that they can show they got the right answer somehow. But when they are actually working on real problems, the theory is that they don't know the answer: the aim of the experiment is to find it out. The good scientist will try again and again, and be prepared for a totally unexpected result. But what if he's sure that he already knows what the result should be? What if current opinion is cast in concrete on that? What if he has a gut feeling himself that that's what it should be? The temptation to think that current opinion and his own instincts must be right, and it's the facts that are wrong, appears to be too much for some people to overcome.

A well-known statistician was reported in the *Daily Telegraph* in August 1992 as stating that the reason why the Japanese, the second heaviest cigarette smoking nation in the world, have a low rate of lung cancer and the longest life expectancy in the world, is that smoking was virtually unknown in Japan before 1948. Apart from the fact that this implies that you have to smoke for fifty years or so before it begins to do you any harm, it isn't true. The Japanese record their social history very carefully, and as explained in the previous chapter, tobacco was introduced in 1542, before it reached most of Europe. In 1906, the first year for which official figures are available, 47 million Japanese smoked 34 billion cigarettes. Since they had a high birth-rate, many of the 47 million must have been too young to smoke, and almost no women did, so this points to a high smoking rate among the men. By 1920 it was estimated that Japanese men, at least, smoked as many cigarettes as the Americans.

In the 1940s and 50s over 80% of Japanese men smoked, but the lung cancer rate was very low. The smoking rate is now down to under 65%, and the lung cancer rate is rising, though it is still lower than in other countries. This is surely because cancer is mainly a disease of the old, and the Japanese live longer than anyone.

People think they know that smoking makes you die young. The Japanese don't die young, so they can't have smoked for long enough. We will meet other examples of this attitude.

3

'Lies, damned lies ...'

We all know that there are 'lies, damned lies, and statistics', whether or not it was Disraeli who first said it. A charming lady at a noted statistical institution, asked to recommend a text to help an amateur on the subject, unhesitatingly said: *How to Lie with Statistics*. It is indeed very useful.

Here are some more sayings to be remembered: 'Round numbers are always false,' said Dr Samuel Johnson, whose massive common-sense helped to build the British character. 'Figures won't lie, but liars can figure,' said General Charles H. Grosvenor, an American politician from Ohio. And Alvan Feinstein, Sterling Professor of Medicine and Epidemiology (the study of the causes of disease) at the School of Medicine, Yale University, one of the world's leading epidemiologists, writing in 1997 on the methods used in that science, spoke of 'the majesty of elegant (and sometimes mysterious) statistics'.

So beware of round numbers plumped down before you without explanation, remember that the world is full of liars, some of them most respectable people, and don't get carried away by elegant and mysterious statistics. But where do all these round numbers, these figures, these mysterious statistics actually come from?

First of all they come from death certificates. More of those later. Then there are the various scientific studies. The finest guide to these is a little work called *Science Without Sense*, subtitled *The Risky Business of Public Health Research*, by Steven Milloy. It is as useful as *How to Lie with Statistics*.

There are two basic kinds of epidemiological studies: cohort and case-control. Cohort studies are difficult. They involve identifying a group of people to be studied and keeping track of them for a number of years, perhaps even until they die. By that time the public may have lost interest in that particular scare.

Case-control studies are better because they're quick. 'Quick 'n' dirty', says Mr Milloy. You take a group of people who have the disease you're working on, and a matching group who haven't. Then you find what differences in the lifestyle or circumstances of the two groups could account for the differences in health.

Then there are intervention trials, in which you take two groups of people, as alike as possible in lifestyle and circumstances, and make one do something like giving up smoking, changing their diet, taking exercise, and taking drugs for some particular condition, and at the end of a period of time compare their states of health.

An article in the *Lancet* (19 February 1994) states:

> Research on the health of populations is still dominated by experimental designs based on simplistic notions of causality that try to remove the variation and complexity of real-life health and disease process [resulting in] an exaggerated focus on risk factors – any suggested positive or inverse association with the outcome under study – and in the equation of risk with causation. Attribution of causal status to risk factors designed in this way has led to wasteful investment of public money in large intervention trials that are incapable of achieving their stated aims.

'Correlation is not causality' is the catchphrase that should be suspended, written in large red letters, over the desk of every statistician. In Denmark storks are more likely to be nesting on the roofs of houses in which large families live. Any statistician who gathered from this that storks bring babies would be ignoring the above slogan (some have made almost equally wild assumptions). Large families are likely to live in larger houses, with more roof space and more chimneys for the storks to nest by.

In some African countries cancer rates are very low. This doesn't mean that the inhabitants live healthier lives than we do. Cancer is, to repeat, primarily a disease of the old, and the average age of death in these countries is 20 or 30 years below that in Europe and North America. In the 1980s there were apparently no deaths at all of babies in the old Soviet Union. This was because

the infant death rates were rising so alarmingly that the government decided not to publish the figures.

In *What Risk*, Professor Feinstein echoes the *Lancet* above:

> The inadequacy of the science underlying many epidemiological
> studies would be worrying in any discipline but in a discipline that
> self-avowedly seeks to better the world it is of grave concern. The
> *political influences* on and goals of epidemiologists are obvious ...
> [emphasis added].

These goals he lists as instituting (that is, starting), disseminating
(spreading), building into the peer review process (by which any
new scientific work is supposed to be examined by other experts
in the same field); coercing into grant approval (that's to say
persuading government or institutions to give money); and
using as stepping-stones in their careers what he unhesitatingly
describes as very defective methods used in epidemiological
studies.

The first 'defective method' listed by the Professor seems so
obviously absurd that it is difficult to see how it could ever have
arisen: for some prominent epidemiologists, 'the sequence of action
is irrelevant'. Someone may have a disease, be cured, and then
ingest some toxin (or poisonous substance), and the toxin could be
blamed for the disease.

The second he lists is the difficult one of 'confounding factors'. You have a disease that has been put down to the current
fashionable cause. Sure enough, you do whatever it is that it's
politically correct to blame that disease on. But your only sister
died of it, and so did both your parents. You drink heavily, and
that too has been blamed for this disease. You take no exercise,
and eat a heavy diet poor in vegetables and fruit, and that has
been blamed for many diseases. What's more, recent research
has shown that there may well be a virus involved. Yet, says the
Professor from Yale, confounding factors receive insufficient
attention.

'Susceptibility bias', the third in his list, has received almost no
attention. This means that something that might predispose someone to get that disease isn't taken into consideration. You are a
citizen, say, of an Eastern European country that put you, and

many others, into an extremely unpleasant prison for a considerable number of years. When you got out, half-starved and suffering
from the effects of brutal treatment, you lived it up as much as you
could. Who could blame you? Now your present disease is put
down to your self-indulgence.

Then, says the Professor, there is 'detection bias'. This happens
when researchers try harder to find certain ailments rather than
others. This is obviously going to happen when some disease has
received a great deal of publicity, and consequently anyone working on it is more likely to get grants to study it. There is also the
interesting problem that arises when new methods of diagnosis
have identified a large number of cases that would previously not
have been discovered. The headlines shriek of a new epidemic, but
all that is really new is the scanner.

The Professor also warns that death certificates are 'merely a
passport to burial', and should never be used in studies.

Then there is what he calls 'transfer bias'. This comes about in
'case-control' studies, when a study is made of two groups of
people, one of which is thought to be at risk for some reason, and
the other not, as explained earlier. It is obviously very necessary
that the two groups should be as similar as possible, so that the risk
under study is really the only difference between them. This however is not always the case.

Passports to burial

On the subject of death certificates, for instance, there was a report
in *Human & Experimental Toxicology* 13 (1994): 'Accuracy of Admis-
sion and Pre-Autopsy Clinical Diagnosis in the Light of Autopsy
Findings: a Study Conducted in Budapest.' This study, which was
less likely to contain as much lying as some because all its subjects
were dead, showed how often the findings of postmortems contra-
dicted diagnoses made by doctors in the patients' lifetimes. There
is considerable evidence from other sources, showing that the rate
of error can be anything up to 30%, even as much as 50%.

A report by the Royal Colleges of Pathologists Surgeons and
Physicians, 'The Autopsy and Audit' (August 1991), says:

In autopsies [postmortems] on patients thought to have died of malignant disease [cancer] there was only 75% agreement that malignancy was the cause of death, and in only 56% was the primary site identified correctly.

So if you are told that you've got cancer there may be a one in four chance that you haven't, and even if you have there's a slightly less than fifty-fifty chance that you're being treated for one in the wrong place. You may be consoled by knowing that if you are one of the 27% of patients in this country who will enjoy a postmortem after death the truth will emerge. Or will it? The Hungarian study states:

> It should be noted that even when there is agreement between clinical and post-mortem diagnosis in the underlying cause of death this does not necessarily imply complete agreement. Thus of 697 cases of neoplasia [cancers] diagnosed at post-mortem, there was agreement that a neoplasm was the underlying cause in only 636, that it was in the same minor category in only 562, and that it had the correct 3 digit ICD [International Classification of Diseases Code] in over 506.

In fact, the pathologists often couldn't agree on exactly what had killed you even after they'd cut you up.

The threat of clarity

Professor Feinstein warns us, perhaps rather cynically, about this threat in plain words when he discusses risk factors, which can also be called risk ratios, relative risks, rate ratios, odds ratios. His implication seems to be that clarity does not always suit the compilers of such studies. A driving licence is a 'risk factor' for a road accident, in that without one you are not very likely to be driving a car. But it doesn't mean that you are inevitably going to have an accident. Nor does it mean that without one you won't have an accident. Plenty of pedestrians and bicyclists do.

Three hundred risk factors have been identified as present in heart disease. They include age, having English as a mother tongue, being a man, being widowed, not going to church, not being a Mormon, drinking a lot, being a teetotaller, drinking too much milk, drinking too little milk, being rich ('good financial status'), being poor ('low socio-economic status'), snoring, and not eating mackerel. Three hundred in all, covering, you'd think, most of the things that people do, or don't do, or are, or are not.

But even if you are an Englishman who doesn't go to church, isn't a Mormon, drinks too much or too little milk or alcohol, doesn't eat mackerel, and is rich or poor and snores, and the rest of it, this doesn't mean that you are fated to develop heart disease. Of course you may well do so, because it is far and away the commonest disease and cause of death in developed countries, but a risk factor only points to what might happen. And sometimes, as in the case of the storks, it can point in entirely the wrong direction.

There is another extremely important limitation: proper trials are almost impossible if they involve something that is known to be bad for you. You can't expect people to take part in a trial that involves getting half of them to drink pure water and the other half untreated sewage water, in order to determine the health risks. If that happened, the epidemiologists know that they would end up in court. The Nazis were able to do experiments of this kind on prisoners in concentration camps, but as far as we know without any kind of useful result.

Bearing all this in mind, let us look at what statistics are, and what they should be. What they should be are figures carefully collected by people who know what they are doing and are honest and unbiased, based on precise information and definitions, collected from dependable sources, and presented without prevarication or reservations. Let's see what some actual experience of what is grandly called 'fieldwork' could reveal about these 'elegant (and sometimes mysterious) statistics', to quote the excellent Feinstein again.

Say that you have set out to collect statistics on drinking. Do you conduct your inquiries in a pub or at a Salvation Army meeting? You settle for the pub, but you know that in certain circumstances some of your colleagues might go for the other, because it would be much simpler to work on forms with all the 'noes' ticked, if they thought they could get away with it. But you go for the pub. You have a list of fifty pub clients, and fifty of the families of known drinkers.

Six of your fifty pub-goers flatly refuse to answer any questions at all, and are not very polite about it. Two say 'It's my own business'; you wonder whether they have any other business. Seventeen are delighted to talk to you about anything except their drinking habits. Four are speechless. One is being sick outside. Of the fewer than half of your sample remaining, eight pot-bellied, red-nosed, slightly incoherent people state that they never have more than a couple of pints. Three add that it's only at weekends. Seven highly excited, cheerful young people say that they drink anything that's going, and put their average daily consumption at anything up to seventeen drinks of all kinds. Their friends or partners giggle appreciatively. Of the remainder, two say they know they drink too much, but would obviously rather not go into details. Five give precise details of their consumption, but their body language suggests to you that two or possibly three are lying.

So you go to interview the fifty families. Eight of the addresses turn out to be false. You did have your suspicions when one of them was the Tower of London. Thirteen of the people refuse to talk to you, and you lose count of the doors slammed in your face. Twelve of the women say that they have no problems, and they can't think why you've come. You have doubts about their stories, if only from the aspect of the homes, but you can't break down their loyalties. Of the remaining seventeen the complaints about the drinking range from a mild 'mustn't grumble, but ...' to raging paranoia.

You have your report to send in. The only honest report would state that you couldn't reach any conclusions on the data you had gathered, and anyhow you were sure that at least half of the interviewees were lying. But your employer, who has commissioned the survey, may have an agenda. People who commission surveys sometimes have. If you send in the 'wrong' report you may not get any more work from them. So what do you do?

You are a good conscientious interviewer. You do your best to interview all the people you have been told to interview, and you have honestly written down, in your original report, the answers given by those you have been able to contact. But you know that others of the interviewers you work with are not so scrupulous. They may excuse themselves by muttering that their figures are going to be doctored anyhow, or that the work is impossible and no one could get a genuine result. Anyway, they've got a living to earn.

Then, too, you are a good interviewer in that your voice and manner are always conscientiously and carefully neutral. You do your best to give the person interviewed no hint of the answer you expect. This means that you waste time listening to diffuse and often confusing answers. It's easier and less time-consuming to put your questions pointedly so that the answers can be given briskly. You need not alter the wording: the tone of voice, the facial expression, will usually be all that the other needs. This is specially tempting if you already have a good idea of what your employer wants to hear.

From the ridiculous to the still more ridiculous

That was an imaginary survey. Let's look at a real one, on the highly contentious matter of 'passive smoking'. In 1988 the Louisiana State University Medical Center carried out over three months a survey on 'Lung Cancer in Non-Smoking Women'. On 15 August of that year it applied for an interim grant of $17,265 from the Grants Administration Branch of the National Cancer Institute. This was for direct costs, and did not include overheads on subcontracts. The standard method as used here is to identify a sample of women who had died of lung cancer, though they were described as 'never-smokers', and to find out about anything that might have caused the disease.

The first thing that a researcher with many years experience notices about the questionnaire is that it is extremely long, running to 34 pages. Both the interviewer and the interviewee would have been heartily sick of it by about page 15. Bored interviewees take to answering at random, and the 'don't knows' mount. Bored interviewers have more subtle ways of expressing their resentment: they may race through the questions so fast that a bewildering snatch of dialogue may go something like this:

'Were-there-times-when-she-was-in-an-area-filled-with-cigarette-smoke-for-2-or-more-hours-a-week-on-a-regular-basis-when-she-was-in-her-twenties?' all in one breath.

'Wha–?'

'Yes-or-no?'

'I didn't quite get …'

'Were-there-times-when-she-was-in-an-area-filled-with-cigarette-smoke-for-2-or-more-hours-a-week-on-a-regular-basis-when-she-was-in-her-twenties?'

'I suppose she may have been ...'

'Yes-or-no?'

The wretched interviewee is probably being questioned about a time at least forty years before. Lung cancer is rare before the patient's late fifties; cancers in general are commonest after the age of seventy. Since the purpose of the survey (the perils of smoking) is plain, the answers given will very likely reflect the interviewee's own ideas on the subject.

The answer, therefore, if the interviewee is a passionate anti-smoker, will take the form of a hearty 'Yes!' especially if the interviewer is also an anti-smoker and has stressed the 'yes' in one of the ways known to researchers. '*YES!* or (very quickly in a low voice) no?'

The second feature of importance is to avoid making it at all obvious what the survey is about: on the second page the questions about smoking start, and carry on to page 17. If the questions had been worked out a little more cleverly, this purpose would have been masked. The remaining questions are on her diet and where she lived and worked, and could have been scattered through the text in a way that would have obscured the primary purpose, and avoided the appearance of leading questions.

The relatives who can be interviewed are listed as the husband, brother or sister, child, parent, or 'other'. Without going into the matter of what an 'other' could be, let us assume that an interviewer has pinned you down, holding a formidably thick form, and is reading from it:

Q 'Now I would like to ask you some questions about the smoking habits of your (mother's), (sister's), (wife's), (child's), ('other's') family members when she was growing up. Did her father/mother smoke cigarettes, cigars, pipe? How many years did her father/mother smoke in the household when she was growing up?'

A parent or sibling might be able to answer. It is very unlikely that a husband or child could. As to what an 'other' might come with, who's to say?

You then have to say what other household members who lived in the house with your relative for six months or more smoked cigarettes, cigars, or pipe. You're pretty sure that Granny didn't, in the last years she spent with the family. Or did she? After all, you have the impression that she was a fairly bright young thing in the 1920s, when many young women took to smoking. How can you be sure of what she was up to when she spent all those hours alone in her room upstairs? As for Uncle Rupert, he was a violent anti-smoker when you knew him, but a lot of former smokers turn into the bitterest anti-smokers.

A husband is not very likely to cross-question his wife about the smoking habits of her family. A brother or sister might remember, or might not. Younger family members are not usually terribly interested in what the others are doing. You are certainly not going to remember with absolute accuracy the number of years they smoked, or how much, which is another question on the same page.

How many men did your mother sleep with? And when did you last see your father?

You would know how many times your mother had been married, but as for how many 'partners' she had (question on page 5), and whether any of them smoked tobacco, these are not questions to which you as husband, parent, child, sibling, or 'other' are likely to have got a straight answer, even if you did ask them.

Yet on the next page you as husband, parent, child, sibling, or other are expected to know for how many years and how much these partners smoked.

Q 'How many men did your wife/daughter/mother/sister/other live with at various times? Did they smoke cigarettes, cigars, or a pipe? And for how many years? And on average how much a day?'

Perhaps the answer is expected to go like this:

'Let me see – there was Ron, for 2 years. He smoked 20 cigarettes a day. Then there was Ken, who smoked 3 or 4 cigars a day. That was for 18 months. Then there was Don – that only lasted 8 months, and he smoked about 2 packs a day. Sam smoked a pipe .... '

And so on. Where do the people who concoct these surveys come from?

Q 'Now we'd like you to think about other people she shared living quarters with *in her adult life*. Did she ever room with, or share a household for 6 months or more with people we haven't already talked about?'

Then comes the usual list of questions about such people's smoking habits. There are 2 pages (10 questions) on this. There follow 4 whole pages (46 questions) about up to 8 or 10 of her jobs and whether anyone smoked where she worked.

Is it likely that your mother or sister felt inclined to, or indeed that you'd give her the opportunity to indulge in such detailed reminiscences? 'Oh, shut up, Ma! Who cares that you worked for 6 months in a tax office where your boss smoked 8 cigarettes a day?'

Q 'Other than the circumstances we have talked about, were there times when she was in an area filled with cigarette smoke for 2 or more hours a week on a regular basis when she in her twenties, in her thirties [and so on up to her seventies].'

Here another factor comes into play. If she was a politically correct anti-smoker, then she might well exaggerate her exposure to smoke.

Then at last (at last!) on page 18 we have questions that might be answered precisely, and be relevant:

Q 'We are interested in knowing about any types of cancer that may have occurred in her immediate family.'

This could point to genetic, infectious, or environmental agents in the course of the disease, and is such an obviously sensible question – and one so comparatively easy to answer, because people usually know what their close relatives died of (or were supposed to have died of) – that you wonder how it ever got into this survey.

Then we have her eating habits. By this time (page 19) it is safe to assume that both interviewer and interviewee are thoroughly sick of the whole thing, unless of course the interviewee is being paid, in which case an entirely new element is being introduced. If they look forward to the cash, interviewees are pleased, and may be showing this by trying to give the answers they sense are wanted. The interviewer only wants to get it all over with, and shows in various ways that a quick answer is preferred. Those of the type:

> 'Now let me think. I do believe that she started a new diet in the seventies – or was it the early eighties? No, it was '79. I'm not sure how long she kept it up – not for very long, I fancy, because at Christmas that year she ate the usual dinner with us – or was that in '80? I know she ate a lot of cabbage –.'

are fairly ruthlessly cut short. The interviewee is brought to heel, and falls back on simple 'yes' and 'no'.

The great string bean mystery

At this point the interviewer is given this arcane instruction:

> IF A FOOD IS EATEN SEASONALLY, OBTAIN INFORMATION ON THE FREQUENCY DURING THE SEASON, DURATION OF SEASON, AND THE FREQUENCY FOR THE REMAINDER OF THE YEAR; LATER CONVERT TO FREQUENCY FOR ENTIRE YEAR

and continues to ask how often various foods were eaten, starting with peaches, apricots, nectarines (how often did *your* mother eat a nectarine?) and going on to more than 90 other foods, including various kind of potatoes, hamburgers, spaghetti, peanuts, and chicken with the skin on. There is one curious omission: on page 20 Question 8 asks how often she ate beans '*other than string beans*'. Since almost every kind of food you can imagine or eat was otherwise listed, what had string beans done to be left out?

This is haunting. Why were potatoes, yams, peas, carrots, broccoli, cauliflower, Brussels sprouts, spinach, mustard greens, turnip greens, cole slaw, cabbage, sauerkraut, green salad, baked beans, black-eyed peas, kidney beans, lima beans all included, and string beans specifically put into limbo? After all, asparagus, courgettes, swedes, paprikas, artichokes (both French and Jerusalem), celery, watercress, and parsnips were omitted too, but there was no specific exclusion order against them. It could well be that this discrimination against the string bean could poison the whole of the rest of the proceedings for both of those taking part.

On page 27, the interviewer must ask:

Q 'How often did your relative usually *eat* (*sic*):
Milk, soft drinks, beer, wine, liquor?'

At this, both sides, if awake, could be forgiven for giggling hysterically, unless they were still too troubled about the string beans.

There are, to conclude, some not unreasonable questions about where she lived, and what kind of heating was used in her home. These have some possible relevance, since there is evidence that respiratory disease of all kinds is commoner in towns than in rural areas, and may be linked with various kinds of fuel.

Then you are asked how often your relative had contact with or used:

Q 'paints, lacquers or stains, hair dyes or tints, hair spray, fabric dyes, inks, wood-dust/sawdust, cotton or other textile fibers or dust [what kind of woman, or indeed living creature in the home, has no contact at all with dust?], insecticides or garden sprays, petro-chemical plant emissions, or grain elevator dust.'

In this encyclopaedic gallimaufry of ridiculous and mostly unanswerable questions (did your wife/mother/ daughter/sister ever live with anyone who smoked? Did she eat chicken with the skin on?), there is one unquestioned jewel in the crown, which exposes the absurdity of the whole thing:

Q 'How many months of the year did she keep the windows of her house open during her adult life?'

But there will be people who will still worry most of all about the string beans.

The results of this sort of thing may well be dished out as scientific findings, certified by experts, reprinted in government reports, given in parliamentary answers, made the subject of terrifying articles in the press and even more terrifying television programmes (with pictures of lungs being ripped out); they will produce hysteria from ASH and other anti-smoker campaigning groups, provoke demands for further legislation aimed at the smoker, inspire declarations from the EU (leading, they hope, to some justification for the salaries of the bureaucrats framing the regulations); and they will be made use of in law courts to claim huge sums of money for 'victims of passive smoking'.

Even if the interviewers were omniscient, the interviewees absolutely honest people gifted with the power of total recall, and the late subjects of the inquiry in the habit of telling their families all the tiniest details of their lives (and the families of listening to them), it is difficult to see how the results of such a survey could establish a link between cancer and anything at all.

The average man – poor soul

Statistics are always looking for the average. 'The average drinker has X number of drinks a night.' 'The average smoker loses Y number of years of life.' 'The average motorist has Z number of accident risks.' The trouble is that there isn't usually an average anything in the usual meaning given to the word. If half the drinkers have 2 drinks a night, and the other half 10, no one actually has 6, yet that in the popular view will be the average. It isn't; it's the 'mean', which is what you get here if you add up all the drinks and divide the result by the number of drinkers. You could also have a 'median', which would tell you that half the drinkers have more than that, and the other half less. Or you could use the 'mode', which would take the number of drinks drunk by the greatest number of people. In this case it would not be possible, because we have exactly equal numbers of 10-drink drinkers and 2-drink drinkers. That is, however, not at all likely (see Dr Johnson's warning, above). Say that 52 had only 2 drinks, and 48 had 10. Then your modal figure is 2. But that is not going to take away from the uncomfortable fact that quite a lot of people have had a great deal more to drink than is really good for them or those around them. It is, however, nicely hidden in the 'mode', if that is the figure you want to use.

The 'average' shoe size of women might be five and a half. But no shoe manufacturer would think it a good idea to make shoes only in that size. The 'average' house price in a town might be £80,000. But no estate agent is going to put up all the houses in the area for sale at that price.

In fact no one is ever actually 'average', whether as a drinker, a consumer, or a voter. It suits politicians of certain persuasions to think there is, because they like to deal with the concept of the 'average man' or the unspecified 'people'.

Another popular form of creative statistic-making is to give them in the shape of an unsupported percentage. You have a 25% greater chance of something, usually something unpleasant. It can sound, and is often meant to sound, very alarming. But it means nothing at all unless you know what the overall chance is. If your chance of being struck by lightning is one in 50 million, increasing that chance by one quarter, bringing it down to one in 40 million, which is what 25% is in this case, isn't very worrying, apart from the fact that such slender chances are impossible to calculate.

Responsible statisticians won't accept 'risk ratios' (the technical term for the proportionate difference) of less than a doubling of the risk, which can be shown as 2.0 or 200%, and some would demand at least 300%. Anything under that is described as 'weak'. There is always too much of what is called 'background noise': the possibility of error, confounding factors, miscalculation, and plain lying.

And if you are simply told that there is a 25%, i.e. 1 in 4, chance of something happening, you might be forgiven for translating it into the notion that there is a 3 in 4 chance that it won't happen.

But – a very big but – you must keep your grip on the laws of chance and probability. If you flip a coin 10 times, you won't often get a neat 5 heads and 5 tails. You may get 4 of one and 6 of the other, or 3 and 7, or even 10 and nought (if that happens often, find out where you got the coin from). Even the most extreme odds may not mean anything: it's just the way the chance goes.

So, to augment their risk ratios, statisticians use 'confidence intervals'. You might see a risk ratio expressed as '2.4 (0.8 – 7.2)'.

This means that though the risk ratio is strictly speaking 2.4, anything between 0.8 and 7.2 is within the range of the results of the study. You will see lots of risk ratios showing that people doing something politically incorrect have a three times greater chance of having something nasty happening to them. You will not see the confidence interval, so you do not know whether in fact it has such a wide range that the alarming figure means nothing. If the lower figure in the confidence interval is below one, the risk ratio is not 'statistically significant', so don't worry about it.

If someone throws one of these figures at you ('You have a three times greater chance of having your teeth fall out than I have because you do something politically incorrect and I don't'), ask them what the 'confidence interval' is. With any luck they won't have the faintest idea of what you're talking about.

The confidence interval itself isn't foolproof. The usual confidence interval is of 95%, so that there is only a 1 in 20 chance of its being wrong. Many a sad punter on certainties will tell you all about that. A 90% confidence interval will mean you have a 1 in 10 chance of being wrong. This has been used recently by the American Environmental Protection Agency in surprising circumstances (see pp. 96-7).

Chalk and cheese

Another useful device used by statisticians is the comparison between two groups that look similar but aren't. Suppose, for example, that the annual death rate in the armed forces in peacetime is a mere 20 per 10,000, while among civilians it is 150 per 10,000. You're safer in the forces, see? But the armed forces include almost exclusively healthy young people, while among the civilians are all the old and sick.

Say you want to show whether a diet rich in organically produced fruit and vegetables is good for you. So you identify a group of people who follow this diet and show that they are indeed healthier than those who don't. But organically produced fruit and vegetables are expensive. People who eat them are usually appreciably better off than most of us. They live in better housing, in healthier areas, and are likely to have better medical care, and to be generally better educated and to have more interesting jobs.

This last factor seems to have an important effect on health. A revealing survey on civil servants in London showed clearly that the higher the grade the better the health and the longer the life. Yet the lower grades could hardly be said to be in any way deprived. They have secure jobs and adequate salaries. They all have homes, enough to eat, regular holidays, most have cars, all have their indexed pensions to look forward to. This points to the factor that Professor Eysenck has continually emphasised. Central to his approach is that we cannot behave as if body and mind are totally disconnected. Yet time and again we see experts who do just that. Professor Feinstein discusses that too. He describes as very generally known the fact that people who have heart attacks are often tense and driven, with repressed anger and hostility (sometimes not all that repressed, with due respect to the Professor). He points out that:

> Instead of using well-constructed psychometric methods to identify anger, hostility, and tension, epidemiologists have obtained controversial results by using what may be the world's clumsiest and most over-simplified classification of the complexity of the human psyche.

In other words, you're Type A or Type B. Perhaps this is better than being merely the average man.

Don't we all know that if we are very unhappy or worried we are more likely to get ill? 'Don't carry on like that,' said our mothers, 'you'll make yourself ill.' And sure enough we did.

Elegance?

Perhaps this is the right heading under which to introduce graphs. We all know these, because they show lines that are either going up, sometimes alarmingly and sometimes triumphantly, or down likewise. What we don't know unless we're professionals is that you can produce alarming or triumphant results by drawing them out or squashing them together. Suppose the trading figures for your company's business show a slow, undramatic rise over the years. It won't look much on an ordinary graph. But if you put the vertical lines that show the months or years much closer together, your rise will look much more satisfactory. If you want a less dramatic rise (or fall) just set the lines further apart. You can, too, close up or widen the horizontal lines to show a corresponding result that gives what you are plotting a more or less exciting aspect.

Or you can doctor bits of the graph. You can cut off bits that don't suit your argument. A good example of this, quoted in *Health Scare: The Misuse of Science in Public Health Policy* by J.R. Johnstone & Chris Ulyatt (Australian Institute for Public Policy 1991) is a graph showing the rise in accidents after the drivers had been drinking. Unluckily for the agenda of those who commissioned the work, it showed clearly that drivers who had had one or two drinks before driving had a slightly lower accident rate. This showed up well on the original graph, with an appreciable dip in the line. So this dip in the line was raised a little, and smoothed out, and finally the first section of the graph, which showed the dip, was cut off.

Then there is the pictorial graph. This usually shows little figures of men or women ('the people'), arranged in neat rows. Each figure stands for so many people. Or it could be cars representing so much traffic, or cows so many cows. It is not so easy to do much with these. The little figures are very clear. But if you decide instead to draw one little figure for so many people, and one twice the size for double that number, then you can do something. The larger figure is twice as tall, but then he looks really anorexic. So you, obviously, flesh him out sideways. Now he is twice as tall as the other, and twice as fat. But this makes him look eight times as big. This could be particularly useful for figures on employment, or higher education, but not for hospital waiting lists.

There is also the bar chart which shows solid blocks side by side. By squashing the horizontals so that the differences, though in fact tiny, make the rises, or falls, look much larger, you can make the impression you want. A bar representing only a small difference then looms over the others on the chart.

There are many other things you can do with statistics, if you bear in mind the argument that you can't 'prove' a negative statistically, or indeed scientifically in general. All you can do is disprove something.

Take a very obvious statement: 'All swans are white.' You can't prove that, because someone, somewhere, could find a swan that was black. You can say that since no one has yet, so far as you know, found a black swan, there is a strong probability that all swans are white. That doesn't have the resounding ring of the positive statement, but it is in fact scientific, and the other isn't. Only when someone appears with a black swan can the statement be disproved.

In January 1993 the journal *Iatrophon*, published by IATROS, an international organization of doctors, wrote:

> How do you 'prove' something scientifically? The answer is that you don't. It is possible to prove propositions in mathematics, but not in science. That's the difference between an abstract world and the messy real one. Use of the term 'scientific proof' or 'statistical proof' means that the speaker is ignorant of science or statistics. What science and statistics try to do is to *disprove* things. In statistics, it is always the same thing: the null hypothesis, which states that Group A and Group B are essentially the same ('there's nothing going on here'). The idea is to cast enough doubts on the null hypothesis so that you reject it. ['Look, this swan is definitely black.']

'How much doubt you need to cast,' *Iatrophon* continues, 'is basically an arbitrary decision.'

It is an arbitary decision what to survey when you do do a survey, and how you choose the people to question or study. It is an arbitrary decision how you phrase your questions. It is an arbitrary decision how you decipher the answers you get, and what you finally write down. It is an arbitrary decision how you present your figures and your graphs or charts.

Of course there are many very honest and conscientious researchers whose decisions are made in an irreproachable fashion. But all too often these don't come up with any startling results, simply because the whole subject is so very complex, and the honest worker in the field sometimes has to admit that the honest answer may be a plain 'I don't know.' And this doesn't make headlines. Nor does it get you grants to continue your studies. If an institution, government or private, forks out money for a study, it wants to see some kind of return. A ten-year study on a few hundred or a few thousand people is expensive, and the people who've paid for it don't want to be left with something that won't get their names into the papers.

So there must always be a temptation to remember the ancient statistical law: 'If you torture the data long enough they will confess', and to set about torturing the data in the ways described above. No doubt the experts know of many more such little refinements.

People

And never forget that people tell lies, some quite deliberately, and some because they are unaware of the truth. Remember the little story told by a correspondent writing in the *Lancet* in 1957:

> Yesterday the morning post brought an innocent looking letter from the MRC [Medical Research Council] 'Dear Doctor: in 1951 you stated that you smoked an average of 3 cigarettes a day ....'
> 'Why, you hypocritical old .... '[said the doctor's wife]
> 'How could I,' [the doctor himself] began brokenly, 'How could I say such a thing?'
> 'My husband [says the wife] is a heavy smoker, except when Giving up Smoking. This happens three or four times a year.... Clearly the questionnaire had caught him while he was Giving up Smoking, or, more accurately, Tapering Off. There it is: 3 cigarettes a day, all tabulated, analysed, with confidence limits and the rest of it. It makes you think. I mean, statistical methods are so reliable these days. Isn't it appalling that they have to depend on people?'

They do depend on people. They depend on the people who have ordered the work, and whose motives may be of the very highest, or may not be. These people may be as unprejudiced as it is possible for human creatures to be; they may be honestly unaware of their prejudices and presumptions; they may be entirely cynical and merely think to themselves: 'Well, I've got to live, and this is the way to get grants.'

They depend on the people who do the field-work, who may be honest, efficient, well-informed, impartial, and able to judge the quality of the responses they are getting, or they may be only some, or none, of these. They in turn depend on the people studied, who may be perfectly straightforward and truthful, well-informed and balanced, or may not be.

And above all they depend on the predominant culture of the time, whatever it may call itself: Orthodoxy, Respectability, Con-

formity, Political Correctness, the Will of the People: the mood of
the moment, in fact. We are all affected by it, whether we know it
or not. Orthodoxy fulminates against heretics, respectability and
conformity ostracise them, political correctness does both, and the
will of the people, given its head, has a final solution for them.
Perhaps it is fortunate for us all that there are still some members
of the awkward squad about, with hackles that rise automatically
in the presence of any of the above.

They will tell you that if you have to evaluate a report on any
subject, the first thing to do is to ask yourself: 'Is this orthodox/re-
spectable/conformist/politically correct?' If it is, pull it to pieces.
You are very unlikely to get any surprises. We all know what
they're going to say. If it isn't, accord it some startled respect, and
then pull it to pieces. You may well have an agreeable surprise.

4

The big kill – a big lie?

It is only to be expected that once the anti-smoker movement got going, it would make use of statistics. Statistics as we know them are made for just such movements.

Let us start with a publication that came out in 1985, *The Big Kill*, published by the Health Education Council jointly with the British Medical Association. This document of 15 volumes, one for each regional health authority and one for Wales, declared that smoking killed 77,774 people a year, and put 108,218 people in hospital.

The first question, of course, if you have read the previous chapters, is 'How could they possibly be so certain?' Since we know that a substantial number of people are not diagnosed accurately in their lifetimes, and that there can be some doubt even if an autopsy is carried out, it seems extraordinary that they can pinpoint the cause of death down to single units. On this subject, it was said by the Royal College of Physicians, as quoted by Professor Burch in his 'Can Epidemiology Become a Rigorous Science? How Big is the Big Kill?'(*British Medical Journal* 290, 2 March 1985):

> It is not possible to give a precise estimate [that word!] of the proportion of these excess deaths among smokers which are caused by smoking. There can be little doubt [this usually means that there's quite a bit for sure] that at least half of the estimated 31,000 excess deaths among male smokers aged 35–64 in the United Kingdom were due to smoking ....

'Excess deaths' – a pretty concept – more than their fair share? The Royal College goes on to say:

> It would not be unreasonable to attribute [another term to be wary of] to cigarette smoking 90% of the deaths from lung cancer, 75%

of those from chronic bronchitis, and 25% of those from coronary artery disease. These probably conservative [or at least *possibly* not] assumptions lead to an estimate of about 25,000 deaths from these three diseases caused by smoking among men aged 35 to 64.

So in a dozen lines we have three 'estimates', one 'assumption', one 'probably', and a curiously imprecise: 'It would not be unreasonable'. When it comes to women, we have:

But it can reasonably be assumed that at least 40% of the deaths from lung cancer, 60% of those from bronchitis, and 20% of those from coronary heart disease in women aged 35–64 may well be due to cigarette smoking.

Four lines and another assumption and a 'may well be'. Science shouldn't draw dogmatic conclusions leading to far-reaching policy decisions from assumptions and 'may well bes'. We wouldn't care to travel in an aircraft if we were assured that it was assumed that it would land safely, and it might well be that the wings wouldn't fall off in flight.

The late Professor Burch, who criticised this report in the above mentioned article, was a geneticist, biologist, statistician and authority on radiation, and was distinguished in all these fields. He was never afraid of being controversial.

Note that until about 1950 there was a very wide field for the practice of epidemiology. Tuberculosis, smallpox, plague, typhus, cholera and the rest of the terrible list were widespread. Partly because of immunisation programmes and antibiotics, and perhaps more because of improved standards of public cleanliness with water, sewage, and housing, these ancient curses have withdrawn within the borders of countries whose governments cannot or will not use the counter-measures available. Since such governments do not usually encourage the work of epidemiologists, or anyone else who might give their people ideas about a better life, there might seem to be an epidemic of epidemiologists who are running short of diseases suitable for their investigations.

It is very understandable that when the World Health Organisation (WHO) dubbed the widespread custom of smoking an 'epidemic', there were many people eager to agree. Smoking is more widespread than any infectious disease, and tends to be most common in rather nice countries with good standards of living and five-star hotels to stay in for their conferences (which are never held in places like Phnom Penh or Novosibirsk).

Nor are you likely to find yourself having to look at unpleasant places full of sick people, and risk catching something nasty. Instead you spend much time at the aforesaid conferences, with your expenses paid.

Obtain and manipulate

Professor Burch, in the *BMJ* article mentioned above, says:

> The process of reaching sound conclusions about causation is, however, more of a scientific than a medical task. Medical skills are required, of course, to reach an accurate diagnosis of the cause of death and a proper appreciation of limitations in the evidence, but analysis of the resulting statistics calls for familiarity and dexterity with scientific logic. The two skills are not incompatible but they are not always combined in the same person.

He goes on to quote someone who does combine both skills, that distinguished epidemiologist we have already met, who is also an expert statistician, Professor Feinstein, who points out that a 'licensed' epidemiologist:

> can obtain and manipulate the data in diverse ways that are sanctioned not by the delineated standards of science, but by the traditional practice of epidemiologists.

And from the brief description of epidemiology and epidemiologists given above, using their own lingo it would not be unreasonable to assume possibly, that the 'traditional practice of epidemiologists' could probably be estimated to be, in plain words, dicey. In his article Professor Burch goes on to say:

> That these nicely rounded percentages have culminated in the estimated annual toll of 77,774 deaths (55,107 men and 22,667 women), is not without a certain whimsical charm.

'Assumed', 'estimated', 'not unreasonable', 'may well be', 'nicely rounded percentages'; and a result precise down to the last unit: I think many of us would think of a phrase stronger than 'whimsical charm'. Later in the same article he says:

> The calculation of the annual toll to the nearest death from percentages rounded to the nearest five betrays a certain innocence.

Professor Burch must have been a very polite man.

However, with admirable patience he goes on to discuss the American Surgeon General's 1982 report, which includes a passage from his first report on smoking and health published in 1964. It puts over a methodology-cum-philosophy that, Professor Burch says, 'enjoys wide support among epidemiologists'. As such, it's worth a careful look. It states:

> the causal significance of an association is a matter of judgement which goes beyond any statement of statistical probability. To judge or evaluate the causal significance of the association between an attribute or agent and the disease, or the effect upon health, a number of criteria must be utilised, no one of which is an all-sufficient basis for judgement. These criteria include (a) the consistency of the association, (b) the strength of the association, (c) the specificity of the association, (d) the temporal relationship of the association, and (e) the coherence of the association.

Burch remarks on 'the inadequacy of these poorly defined criteria', which is a relief to all those of us who have failed to make any sense of them. He goes on to quote a well-known statistician, Professor Brownlee, who says: 'the way it [the 1964 report] claims the facts are in conformity with the criterion is to flatly ignore the facts.'

Burch also makes a point of the fact that subjective judgement, on which the Surgeon General places repeated emphasis, should play as limited a role as possible in epidemiology as in other sciences. 'For how do we distinguish between judgement and prejudice?' asks Professor Burch.

Judgement or prejudice?

Scientific analysis should surely aim to replace subjective judgement ('I feel it must be so') by objective testing. ('I don't care what you or I or anyone else feels: I'm going to try it out'), and to do away with prejudice as far as is humanly possible.

Of course there are few, if any, people, entirely without prejudice, but at least they can declare their prejudice, so we know where they're coming from, and what their agenda is. Why should only the smokers and those who provide for them be assumed to be acting out of prejudice? Most anti-smokers may have very good practical or psychological reasons for their stand, but they have learnt to try to mask them with scientific or pseudo-scientific language (laced with a great deal of 'assume', 'may', 'might', 'possibly', etc.), and with plenty of talk about their noble task of saving humanity from itself, whether it wants to be saved or not.

In his *Principles of Medical Statistics*, published in 1937, Professor Sir Austin Bradford Hill stated:

> Merely to presume that the relationship is one of cause and effect is fatally easy; to secure satisfactory proof or disproof, if it be possible at all, is often a task of very great complexity.

Hill later collaborated with Sir Richard Doll on an early piece of research into the causes of lung cancer, the Doctors' Survey, which linked smoking with the disease. Faced with their very complex task, how did they go about it?

First of all, they selected a group of people who were in no way representative of the population in general: that is, doctors. Doctors are much better off, to start with. They are better educated than the population as a whole, and above all they receive better, or at least certainly more, medical attention than the general public, because they know where to go and how to demand it. It has been said that doctors are twice as likely to be involved in accidents, three times more likely to be alcoholics or to commit suicide, and many times more likely to take drugs. They may also be more likely to be represented in the Chamber of Horrors than any other comparable group, according to a personal inquiry at Madame Tussaud's.

Hill and Doll sent out a very simple questionnaire to this group which included all the doctors named in the current British *Medical Register*, and 69% replied: that is, slightly more than two in three.

Of self-selected studies in general, Professor Eysenck has stated roundly:

> no relevant conclusions regarding causality can be drawn from studies of this kind.

Only 'randomised' studies (of which more later), in which two matched groups selected by the researchers are compared, can be taken seriously, he says.

Of the Doctors' Survey, Professor Vandenbroucke of Leiden (perhaps the most distinguished medical institution in Europe), said, in an article in the *American Journal of Epidemiology* (September 1990):

> Often I have wondered why medical opinion was so suddenly and massively swayed into accepting the lung cancer – smoking hypothesis in the late 1950s and early 1960s, as described very well by Burnham. The original case-control studies by Wynder & Graham and by Doll & Hill are still used in a famous epidemiologic exercise (according to the oral tradition in the Netherlands, it was originally drafted by Dr M. Terriss), where *they serve as examples of what can go wrong*: biassed ascertainment of exposure, selection of cases and controls from different source populations, poor ascertainment of 'caseness', etc. Moreover, these studies were preceded by a good many others which had not succeeded to move acceptable medical and public opinion by one iota. *Although a convinced non-smoker myself I am afraid that the sudden and total acceptance of smoking as a cause of lung cancer up to the point that a present-day epidemiologist puts his reputation at peril by treating the subject too light-heartedly, is a phenomenon that belongs rather to the sociology of medical science.* [emphasis added]

What the Professor meant by 'selection of cases and controls from different source populations' is that the comparison of death-rates in doctors who had given up smoking was not with doctors who had not given up, but with *members of the general public*, whom we have already seen differed from doctors in many significant ways (particularly in having less money).

'Ill-conducted procedures'

In May 1978 Professor Burch read, before the Royal Statistical Society, a paper: *Smoking and Lung Cancer: the Problem of Inferring Cause*. In the discussion that followed, it was mentioned that in the Doll & Hill study the doctors were asked only their name, address, and age, and their smoking habits. Dr Seltzer of Harvard University remarked on this, saying:

> no other information was obtained from these British doctors. The cohorts were compared and causality inferred with regard to smoking without any consideration of whether the different groups were alike with regard to their characteristics except for the smoking habit. This ill-conducted procedure is not confined to British epidemiologists, for such practices are unfortunately not unknown in the United States and elsewhere.

This should remind us of what Professor Feinstein said about the 'traditional practices of epidemiologists'.

Later in the discussion Dr I.D. Hill of the MRC Clinical Research Centre, perhaps with unconscious pathos, said that he hadn't taken any part in this but he had grown up with it going on all around him (he is the son of the late Sir Austin). He went on:

> This was a postal survey and there was the choice of asking a hundred questions and getting 10% of the forms back, or asking three questions and getting 70% of the forms back. They decided, in the circumstances at that time, they would ask three questions and hope to get 70% of the forms back.

Now these figures quoted above must first of all be seen in the light of the knowledge we already have about the difficulty in establishing any unquestionable figures for any kind of death. And at the time when this study was going on, Heasman and Lipworth surveyed reports from 75 hospitals of the National Health Service in England and Wales, comparing the doctors' diagnoses made in the patients' lifetimes with the results of postmortem examinations. For cancer of the lung they found that doctors had diagnosed 338 cases when the pathologists had found 417; in only 227 cases did the doctors and the pathologists agree.

In fact, 33% of cases diagnosed as lung cancer were wrongly diagnosed, and 46% that were supposed to be something else were actually lung cancer.

Another study by Feinstein and Wells (*Trans. Assoc. American Physicians* 87) found that heavy smokers had a 90% chance of getting their lung cancer diagnosed (not necessarily correctly, of course), while non-smokers had only a 62% chance.

Doll and Hill stated that they sought confirmation of the cause of death from the doctor certifying the death, who, as we have seen, had an almost 50% chance of being wrong, and when necessary from the consultant to whom the patient had been referred, who presumably had a good chance of being wrong too. Presumably a fair number of the patients whose diagnosis was later proved to have been wrong had seen consultants.

Doll and Hill did not mention any postmortems except very briefly and curiously inconclusively:

> In more than half the deaths (56%) there was histological, cytological, or necropsy [postmortem] evidence together with x-ray or bronchoscopic confirmation.

And remember that according to the Hungarian survey there was a very good chance that pathologists would disagree about the actual details of the disease, which presumably would include the primary site. If the cancer has spread to the lung from another primary site, the cause cannot be automatically put down to smoking.

In 1980 a lengthy report was compiled on rates of cancer in the USA. Enormous sums had been spent on 'the war on cancer', yet, as Professor Samuel Epstein later wrote in 'Losing the War Against Cancer', published in the *International Journal of Health Services* (1990), claims that overall cancer survival rates had improved dramatically in recent years were questionable. These claims, Epstein said, were based on 'rubber numbers', and ignored such factors as earlier diagnoses of cancer, which led to apparent longer survival rates, and the over-diagnosis of benign [non-cancerous] tumours.

Epstein went on to describe the work done on this report. He showed that it excluded from analysis those over the age of 65 and blacks, who had the highest, and increasing, cancer rates.

More manipulation

Epstein called this baldly 'manipulation', and it's difficult to see what else he could have called it. He also pointed out that they had claimed that occupation was responsible for some 4% of cancers, which he called 'a wild 4% guess'. They also decided that diet was determinant in some 35% of all cancers.

Now we come to an interesting example of the sort of thing you can do with statistics. On 8 June 1997, the *Sunday Times* published an article stating that the British government's chief medical officer, Sir Kenneth Calman, had approved for publication a report on *Nutritional Aspects of the Development of Cancer*, which stated that 30 to 70% (a very wide spread, but let it pass) of all cancer cases are linked with diet, and further that diet is ten times more important than the effect of occupational causes and of smoking on all cancers.

We know that 90% of all lung cancer deaths are attributed to smoking. In 1986 the US Environmental Agency estimated that radon gas, naturally present in soil containing certain rock formations, could be responsible for up to 30% of all lung cancer deaths. Another recent estimate was that 40% of lung cancer deaths could be attributable to occupation. An unspecified percentage has been put down to diesel exhaust, and more to the keeping of pet birds, drinking coffee, and the rest of it. There is also strong evidence suggesting a distinct ethnic factor in the incidence of the disease.

American Indians smoke considerably more than whites or blacks, yet have about half the rate of the disease. Only about 2% of Chinese women smoke at all, but they have one of the highest lung cancer rates in the world.

So we have 90% plus 30% plus 40% plus 30 to 70% plus further percentages caused by diesel, pet birds, ethnic factors? Many cancer cases must have several different causes – not so much 'big kill' as over-kill.

This sort of thing is reminiscent of the story of the epidemiologist in the US who added up the numbers of people supposed to be suffering from various diseases. The total exceeded the whole population of the country by so much it seemed that not only was everyone ill, but most of them had several diseases at once.

On the question of ethnic factors, there are some very curious disparities. That of the Japanese, the second heaviest smoking nation, with the world's longest life expectancy and a low rate of lung cancer, has already been mentioned. Then there are the Greeks, the world's heaviest cigarette smokers, who for years had the longest life expectancy in Europe, very little below that of the Japanese. Their record has now been overtaken in Europe by the Swiss (the second highest smoking nation in Europe), and the Spaniards, also heavy smokers, and the Swedes, who don't smoke many cigarettes but do smoke cigars.

Does the anti-smoker live longer?

The Americans, in spite of their intense and often successful anti-smoking activities, are at 21 in the life expectancy list, with Central American Costa Rica, the original banana republic. As already mentioned, American Indians have half the lung cancer rate of the less heavy-smoking American whites; and Asians domiciled in the US, who smoke more than the whites (in some groups smoking rates among the men reach 90%) can nonetheless expect to live seven years longer than other Americans.

In *Smoking and Society* Professor Eysenck discusses this question in great detail. He points out that relative risks in different populations vary from 1.2 to 36.0 in men, and 0.2 to 5.3 in women. (The 0.2 figure indicates that smokers were *less* likely to get lung cancer.)

Eysenck quotes the US Surgeon General's 1982 report as saying:

> The relative risk ratio measures the strength of an association and provides an evaluation of the importance of that factor in the production of a disease

and points out that this isn't true. The risk ratio only gives an evaluation of the strength of a factor once its causal effect has been proved – it can't be used by itself to prove the causal relationship. The storks certainly nest on the roofs of the houses where large families live, but you need some more evidence to show this proves that they bring babies.

Eysenck points out that this extraordinary variation can't be explained by the simple smoking-causes-lung-cancer theory. He discusses the possible role of genetic factors as the determining variables, for which he makes a good case.

These wide differences would also fit the virus theory of the disease, in that different populations could be exposed to the infection in differing degrees. American Indians tend to live apart in their reservations, and many of the Asians in the US keep very much within their own communities, by necessity or choice. It is possible that they are less exposed to infection by the general population.

Blood or breeding?

In the endless debate on 'nature or nurture' it is now generally accepted that genetic factors are of very great importance in all individual human manifestations. This was denied for many years by many people, and the controversy rumbles on. Freudians were obliged to deny the power of heredity, because everything had to be explained by upbringing. Babies, as described by an eighteenth-century pedant, were 'little lumps of flesh': according to Freud early upbringing was all that shaped character. Karl Marx preached much the same; only instead of the family he blamed capitalist society.

The opposite view has been strengthened by the studies of identical twins separated at birth. They truly share an identical genetic heritage, and they are often almost comically similar in habits and attitudes. What evidence there is does suggest that the habit of smoking itself may have a genetic element.

Eysenck discusses the apparent enormous increase in cancer, and reminds us that cancer is primarily a disease of the old. Life expectancy in the developed world has risen very sharply, but people have still got to die of something, and the older they are the more likely they are to die of cancer. He also calculates that if you remove this age factor from the statistical computations, the increase disappears. Methods of diagnosis, too, have changed drastically (though not enough, you might think). Cancer, particularly of the lung, was probably greatly under-diagnosed a hundred years ago. Certainly in the past people who coughed and lost weight and were generally poorly were very likely to be told they were 'consumptive'.

What about heart disease, then? It's on the cigarette packet, in capital letters: SMOKING CAUSES HEART DISEASE. The most authoritative study on this is certainly the Framingham Heart Study, which is known as the Rolls-Royce of studies. In this town in Massachusetts, 5,127 men and women have been studied since 1948. They have had the fullest details taken on their health and life-style, and have been checked every two years. Dr Seltzer of Harvard University discusses this study at length in 'Framingham Study Data and "Established Wisdom" about Cigarette Smoking and Coronary Heart Disease', *Journal of Critical Epidemiology* 42, no. 8 (1989).

The results of the study show that there is no relationship between smoking and heart disease in women except a very slight favourable one (women who smoke have a very slightly lower rate of angina, not statistically significant).

For men, the relative risk starts at 1.3 in smokers of forty or more cigarettes a day. Remember, the risk ratio of 2 has been designated the lower boundary of a weak association, so this means in fact a non-significant association. This risk went down to exactly one, that is, no risk at all, as the subjects aged. When information about certain of the other 300 risk factors for heart disease were taken into account, the relationship between smoking and heart disease was lost. Dr Seltzer asks: 'What use did the Surgeon General's report in 1983 make of these results?' and quotes the report as follows:

It starts by declaring that 'cigarette smoking is a major cause of coronary heart disease (CHD) in the US for both men and women.
1. In men, the incidence of CHD is two fold greater in cigarette smokers than in non-smokers and fourfold greater in heavy smokers.

2. In women, the rates of CHD are lower than in men but are commensurately higher when the smoking patterns are similar to those in men.

3. The risk of developing CHD increases with the duration (in years) of cigarette smoking.

4. The cessation of smoking leads to CHD death rates that are substantially lower in the stopped smokers than are in the continuing smokers, and after 10 years of non-smoking, the CHD incidence of former light smokers approximates those of non-smokers.'

One can only admire such a creative usage of statistics and epidemiology.

Middle-aged at 69?

In a letter to *The Times* in July 1994, a much-quoted popular statistician stated that 50,000 people per year in Britain died 20 or 25 years before their time because of their smoking.

In that year the average expectation of life for men was 72 years, and for women 78. If smokers were losing '20-25 years of life', the men would have died at ages between 47 and 52, and the women between 53 and 58. The official statistics gave the latest (1992) available figures, which are given at five-year intervals, so that the deaths were in a longer period of time. Deaths in England and Wales *from all causes* between the ages of 45 and 54 for men were 13,117, and for women between 50 and 59 were 12,305, a total of 25,422. Even when the much smaller figures for Scotland and Northern Ireland are added, the total is nearer half the statistician's, and remember that this is of all deaths, and for a longer period of time. The specific figures for cancer of the lung, trachea and bronchus were 1,164 for men, and 984 for women. (Remember that a certain number of these were certainly misdiagnosed, though we don't know whether that would leave us with more or fewer genuine cases.) For all heart and circulatory system diseases, the numbers were 5,294 for men and 2,996 for women. Even if all these deaths were of smokers, and all can be attributed to their smoking and nothing else, the total is just over 10,000.

However, it must be remembered that expectation of life rises as you age, so that a man who reaches the age of 60 in one piece can expect to live another 18 years, and a woman 22. It is said that on average people who die between 35 and 69 do so at 62, so you can say they've lost 18 years of life. But it is also necessary to take into account the fact that many people who die prematurely do so because their parents did; that is, there is an inherited family predisposition. Many diseases have at least a strong hereditary factor in them, and so do psychological traits that, as Professor Eysenck has shown, can certainly affect your health.

In a report published in the *Lancet* in 1992, it was said that half of smokers died in middle age, which was defined as ending at the age of 69. The question of the definition of the ages has shifted so much with the much longer life expectancies in this century that there is some variation in the figures usually given. People asked tactfully what they'd call the end of middle age give 55 or 60. Pushing it to the extreme, one might say 65, men's retirement age. Politicians, and some others, tend to see 45 as still 'young'. WHO figures state that at 65 you can expect 13 more years of life, which would give us a 'youth' of 45 years, middle age of 20 years, and old age of 13 years. This looks much out of proportion, and 70 as the onset of age makes it still more so.

Much as some of us may be flattered by the thought that we're only a few years removed from lusty middle-age, surely there are not many 68 or 69-year-olds who would have the face to describe themselves as middle-aged.

There is also the figure put out by anti-smoker bodies in the UK in recent years, that 300 smokers died a day. This sounds awful enough, until you ask how many people die a day anyhow. The figure for the year in which this was being said was some 620,000, i.e. about 1,700 a day. But smokers are about 30% of the population. The 300 only represented about 17%. The figure as given could mean only that 13% of smokers weren't dying at all.

When this was kindly pointed out, the anti-smoker organisations concerned switched, without explanation or apology, to saying that the 300 died of 'smoking-related diseases'. But there are a very large number of diseases described as 'smoking-related'. Cancer and heart disease accounted for some 400,000 of the 620,000 total. Many non-smokers must have died of them too.

To return to the heart disease question, Eysenck, in *Smoking and Society*, deals with this at some length. He discusses, as with cancer, the genetic possibilities, and the large part played by stress and other psychological factors. His reasoning appears to be common-sensical, and difficult to refute, and in fact has never been adequately responded to at all. There are also the 300 risk factors previously described, and recently some work has been done on the role of an infection, a bacterium causing damage in childhood that results in heart trouble later in life.

But surely, you may say, this question could be settled easily enough. With all these studies being done, couldn't someone do an 'intervention trial', as described in *Science without Sense*, comparing two groups of smoking and non-smoking people. The answer is that this has indeed been done. There have been a number of studies that have done something like that. But you've never heard of them? When you hear about the results obtained you will see why.

There has been only one that dealt solely with smoking. This was the first 'Whitehall' study, starting in 1968, which recruited 1,445 British civil servants. Half were encouraged to give up smoking, the others were left alone. After a year smoking in the intervention group (the nagged) was down by 75%. After ten years, 17.2% of this group was dead, as against 17.5% of the control group. This difference in percentage is not statistically significant.

There was no difference in deaths from lung cancer or heart disease, and the only other unexpected result was that the intervention group had 28 deaths from cancer other than lung cancer, compared with the control in which the number of deaths from such cancers was 12. This is statistically significant.

Another study, with a wider range, was the 'Multiple Risk Factor Intervention Trial' (MRFIT) in the US. In this there were 12,866 subjects. They were all shown to be at risk of heart disease because of their lifestyle and their general health. (With 300 risk factors that's not surprising.) One group was given drugs for high blood pressure, encouraged to eat more healthily, and to stop smoking. The other was left alone, as in the Whitehall study.

These were not self-selected studies, and seem to have been conducted competently. At the end of the MRFIT study, 41.2 per thousand of the 'healthy' group were dead, as against 40.4 per thousand of the other.

Scientists investigating the study didn't like these results, and went over them again. They found that the drugs to reduce high blood pressure had in fact increased the death rate among the men given them, and were forced to conclude that the risk factors had nothing to do with the actual risks.

Professor Burch, in a letter to the *British Medical Journal* (March 1985) pointed out that in these two studies:

> in the low smoking intervention groups 56 cases of lung cancer were recorded in a total starting population of 7,142 men (0.78%); the corresponding number for the more heavily smoking normal care groups being 53 in 7,169 (0.74%). Findings for cancer other than those of the lung were even more surprising. Some 88 cases (1.23%) were recorded in the low smoking intervention groups, but only 60 cases (0.84%) in the normal care groups. Thus in the category 'all cancers' there were 144 cases (2.02%) in the intervention groups but 113 cases (1.58%) in the more heavily smoking normal care groups. Reduced levels of smoking were associated with increases in cancer incidence.

He concludes:

> It is fair to ask experts to explain why these remarkable findings from methodologically reputable trials conflict so drastically with their claims.

Professor Burch adds, in *Can Epidemiology Become a Rigorous Science?*

> Strenuous efforts have been made to rescue something from the wreckage, though Stallones risked the creation of many personal enemies when he wrote: 'No amount of squirming on the hook alters the fact that for every 1,000 test subjects 41.2 died and for every 1,000 control subjects 40.4 died.'

'Many personal enemies' for pointing out the obvious?

Squirming on the hook

The Finnish businessmen's study in the 1980s took 612 48-year-old businessmen and got them to do what was done in MRFIT: change their diet, give up smoking, and take various drugs to reduce blood pressure. They also made them take more exercise.

The control group was of 610 similar men, all 48-year-old business men with as far as possible similar habits and life-styles. This is what is called 'randomisation'. It doesn't sound random: in essence it means that the subjects and the controls are chosen from similar people by the investigators; unlike the self-selected smokers and non-smokers in the Hill & Doll study.

After the allotted period of 15 years, it was found that the healthy-livers had totted up 67 deaths, and the others only 46. There was no squirming on the hook about this because it was ignored. And that is the method now used with any evidence that conflicts with the accepted version. The deadly effects of smoking have now entered folklore. There is no need for the medicine men to debate anything. The sun goes round the earth, and if you dare to disagree, nobody's going to speak to you, so there. And you're not going to be asked to served on any official bodies, either.

Another very good example of this sort of attitude was with the Australian government's health survey (1989-90 National Health Survey Lifestyle and Health Australia, Australian Bureau of Statistics, Catalogue No.4366.0, Ian Castles, Australian Statistician). We tend to think of the Australians as manly and tough, a view put across in such amusing films as *Crocodile Dundee*, but about smoking they have become almost Californian in their alarm about the habit. But then, we once thought the Americans were manly and tough.

Yet in this government survey, in which there was no question of finance by any interested parties, or any pro-smoking bias, and in which 22,000 families were studied, it came over quite clearly that smokers were on the whole in better health than non-smokers, and definitely better than ex-smokers.

This surely sensational news was not mentioned in the British media at all, except for two articles in the quality press, one by Professor Eysenck in the *Sunday Telegraph* and the other by Lord (Woodrow) Wyatt in *The Times*.

There was a similar result to a similar survey in France (CRE-DES study 1988-90), described in *Tabac: l'histoire d'une imposture*, an admirable little work, witty as only the French can (still) be. This too found smokers in better health. So, very interestingly indeed, did the US government study (*Cigarette Smoking and Health Characteristics*, from the National Center for Health Statistics, July 1964 – June 1965), at least as far as moderate smokers were concerned.

This last study is particularly noteworthy because it came at the start of the anti-smoker movement in the US, and though its tone generally is commendably fair, it does make the most of such figures as seem to support the PC case. Nevertheless, it is one of the few such studies that takes into account the amount smoked, and shows that people who smoke what anyone would call heavily have more problems than those who smoke moderately, which indeed is what might be expected. It is reasonable to think that anyone who smokes 50 or 60 a day may have more problems to start off with.

You haven't heard of any of these? You won't have. The only reference, apart from the two authoritative articles mentioned above, was a grouchy remark, on the Australian study, that the people were all 'self-diagnosed': that is, their word was taken for it whether they were ill or not. But after what you now know about doctors' diagnoses, surely the patients had just as much chance of being right. In any case, they would know whether they felt ill, and what their doctors had said about it, and whether they themselves thought they were ill or not. If the favourable result proved only that smokers were less likely to be hypochondriacs, that would surely say something positive about 'the bastards'. And it should be remembered that not only are hypochondriacs a nuisance to their doctors, their families, their friends, and the NHS; they can also be a danger to themselves.

There was a study in Heidelberg, described by Professor Eysenck in *Psychological Reports* (1989) in which 528 men who smoked were asked whether they, as smokers, were convinced that they would be very likely to develop lung cancer, heart disease, or other 'smoking-related diseases'. The 72 who answered 'yes', while admitting that their views were taken from information in the media, had an almost three times higher death rate at the end of 13 years than those who were not so influenced.

Fear can kill. This has been known since disease was first studied. We are entitled to wonder how many people have been killed more by the fear of 'smoking-related diseases' than by any actual disease itself.

Certain efforts have been made to find out where some of the figures on 'smoking-related deaths' have come from. When Baroness Jay reported to the House of Lords (24 July 1997) that the number of smoking-related deaths in the UK was 120,000, she admitted that 'smoking is not recorded on the death certificate and analysis is not available at individual death level'. It is difficult to see how any real estimate of the actual deaths can be made. It is also odd that the Royal College of Physicians gave the number of deaths as 50,000 in 1984, since when smoking has decreased considerably, while 'smoking-related deaths' have more than doubled. Ah, the experts say, the deaths relate to the higher smoking rates of years before, since these diseases take a long time to develop (in Japan, remember, some 49 years). Yet the smoking rate was dropping for years before 1984. Why didn't the deaths in that year reflect the earlier higher rate of smoking?

Ask a silly question

In the US, as in Britain, death certificates do not record anything like smoking (except in a very few states where about 3% of deaths are described as 'smoking-related'). The official figure of 'smoking-related deaths' there is 450,000, or 470,000, or 500,000, according to whom you believe.

Dr Bernard M. Wagner, editor of *Modern Pathology*, in May 1996 told of the experiences of a *Detroit News* reporter, Nickie McWhirter, who dared to ask: 'Is it true that 435,000 Americans die every year from smoking-related illnesses?' (This was the number circulating in her circles, apparently.) She was told to contact the local American Lung Association office, but they didn't know. Then she was told to contact the National Center of Health Statistics, a branch of the National Center for Disease Control, and given a telephone number, but it didn't help because they didn't know. Several telephone calls round several different wrong civil service numbers later, she contacted someone in Statistical Resources at yet another department, who said that his office collected mortality based on death certificates. The data is categorised by race, sex, age, and place, but not by smoking. So he didn't know. Our heroine refused to give up. She tracked the Office of Smoking and Health to its office in Atlanta. The public information officer said the 435,000 figure came from its computers based on formulas specially programmed for 'smoking-related stuff', as he put it. She asked him how, if no lifestyle data on individual patients and their medical histories are collected, the computer can possibly decide whether deaths are smoking-related. He didn't know. She was given the number of the Operations Manager of SAMMEC, the computer programme Smoking Attributable Morbidity, Mortality, and Economic Cost, who explained that the computer is fed raw data and SAMMEC uses various intricate mathematical formulas to determine how many people in various age groups, locations, and other categories are likely to get sick or die from what diseases and how many of these can be assumed to be smoking-related.

We're back to 'assumed'. The manager confirmed that no real people, living or dead, are studied, no doctors consulted, no environmental factors, or presumably any others, are considered. He waxed lyrical about SAMMEC and what it could do, provided it is fed the appropriate SAFs. These are the 'smoking-attributable fraction' for each disease or group of people studied; they are derived from a mathematical formula. The reporter demanded to know whether at any time some human being looked at other human beings, talked to their doctors, somehow gathered enough information from reality to begin to devise a mathematical formula that might be applied to large groups of people much later, without needing to study those people. The manager didn't know.

He thought the original work was part of work done by A.M. and D.E. Lilienfeld in their *Foundations of Epidemiology* (OUP, 1980). Mr Lauren A. Colby, an American lawyer, author of an interesting short study, *In Defense of Smoking*, says it isn't.

No real people, living or dead, are studied. Figures are studied (and estimated, and assumed, and cause-coded, and the rest of it): people never.

Heil the computer ....

Wanted – a victim

Some years ago, I made a prediction ... I said that the anti-smoking movement had a big problem ... even if smoking really were so harmful to smokers as was claimed, the natural response would be to call it a matter of individual choice .... The only solution to this problem, I said, would be for it to find – and this was my term – an 'innocent bystander' The ideological function of this search for innocent bystanders has been crucial.

Thus Peter Berger, Professor of Sociology at Boston University, in 1991. Or as Mr Des Wilson, of PAT ('Parents Against Tobacco'), wrote in an article in *The Times* (9 January 1990):

The problem with the obvious alternative [to health education, which he admits is not entirely effective] – much tougher controls – is that it tends to be opposed even by non-smokers who believe that in a free society people should be able to choose whether to smoke or not. The campaign being launched today by 100 well-known parents to protect children from smoking could represent the most effective approach yet, for it circumvents the 'free to choose' obstacle.

Therefore it leads, one presumes, to the possibility of imposing Mr Wilson's 'much tougher controls'. Notice that he defines freedom of choice as an 'obstacle'.

Of course Professor Berger was quite right about the response of the smokers: which boiled down to a more or less polite 'Mind your own business!' But that is what antis of all kinds can't do. Whether they haven't got any real business of their own to mind, or whether they get more pleasure out of minding other people's, that is what they choose to do.

The assault then switched away from the danger to smokers to the nuisance that smokers were to others with their 'filthy' smelly smoke. Smokers were able to retort that a lot of people were nuisances to others: people who did not use deodorants, did use powerful aftershave and hair lotions not of the highest quality, drank a lot of beer or cheap wine, did not wash themselves or their clothes much, and ate garlic, sometimes all at once. You can't say: 'Please put out your garlic!' or 'Kindly take your armpits into the garden!' The smoker has to suffer in silence; let the others endure his smoke, which does at least mask some of the other horrors. So, as Professor Berger says, a victim was necessary, and one was duly found, the Passive Smoker.

The first of these unfortunates seems to have been a mouse. It was, however, not a very convincing victim, for E. Lorenz et al. (in *Cancer Research* 3 [2]: 1943) found no evidence of harm done to mice exposed to cigarette smoke for up to 693 hours. This was before this century's great smoking witch-hunt had got under way, except of course in Nazi Germany.

Passiver Zigarettenrauchbeatmung

Once it had got going, the 'evidence' started to come in, from various sources, but the epithet itself seems to have been used first, appropriately, in Germany, in 1963, when an article by H. Otto in the *Frankfurter Zeitschrift fuer Pathologie* was entitled: 'Experimentelle Untersuchungen an Maeusen mit passiver Zigarettenrauchbeatmung'. So there is our passive smoking, apparently for the first time.

It was at the Third World Conference on Smoking and Health set up by the World Health Organisation in New York in 1975 that the subject was first discussed. WHO is part of the United Nations Organisation that has not escaped the criticisms levelled at that body, and has attracted others peculiar to itself. B.J. Cutler, foreign affairs correspondent for Scripps Howard News Service, said in the *Washington Times* (30 May 1990):

> It suffers from the same maladies as other international agencies: a bloated bureaucracy, too many conferences, and a plethora of programs that detract from what should be its focus – meeting the health needs of the world's poorest people. Once a year WHO's

bureaucrats and delegates meet in Geneva and once a year, America's leading expert on WHO mismanagement issues a damning paper timed to coincide with the conclave.

In his list of horrors, Mr Dietrich points out that each WHO assembly costs $2.5 million – more than twice as much as the organisation spends annually to fight malaria in Africa. Two-thirds of its staff work in comfy offices in attactive European or US cities. It spends twice as much per head on very rich countries like Saudi Arabia and Singapore as on the world's poorest, Ethiopia, which got a total of 5 cents per person in 1989. Out of its 1990-91 budget of $1.4 billion, WHO can find only $500,000 dollars (0.036%) to fight the leading child killers in South East Asia, namely respiratory infections. This amounts to less than one penny per child.

Thirty-four million people

At one of these WHO conferences, in New York in 1975, a delegate cited the case of one patient who 'became so tight with wheezing and asthma that she could not get her breath' while working in an area where smoking was allowed. From this one case, for which he did not give any medical evidence, he went on to draw a heart-rending picture of approximately 34 million others for whom the problem is real and extremely serious. He gave no evidence for this either, apart from quoting information on carbon dioxide supplied by a researcher whose conclusions on passive smoking had been questioned by two American government agencies.

Tobacco smoke has not been proved to be an allergen, that is, capable of causing allergic reactions. At yet another conference in 1979, two researchers referred to a report showing that Swedish asthmatic patients had a positive (bad) reaction to skin testing with tobacco leaf extract. This is not the same as breathing tobacco smoke. No doubt there are many plants that mixed up and applied to the skin would prove irritating. This was emphasised in an article by a Swedish colleague, significantly entitled 'Tobacco Allergy – Does it Exist?' in *Laekatidningen*, 1980.

American researchers reported on discomfort felt by asthmatics exposed to very high levels of smoke, which were recognized as unrealistic by the researchers themselves. Also they did not do what is usual in such studies: find non-asthmatics who could be similarly tested, to compare the effects. Two more researchers reported that they had found non-smokers exposed to smoking (unspecified) in their work-places for twenty years who had 'lower values of small-airways function'. However, critics pointed out that there was no evidence that this meant anything at all, or did anyone any harm, and wondered where the original researchers had found a typical group of workers who had never been exposed to smoke for twenty years for the necessary comparison. Four more studies showed no relationship between passive smoking and respiratory disease. This didn't stop complaints about it growing in number and shrillness. Nor has the fact that smoking in the UK has dropped from over half of the population to about a third in twenty-five years prevented the number of cases of asthma from doubling in that time.

In fact, smoking used to be prescribed for asthmatics. There are still asthmatics who insist that smoking relieves their symptoms. It is a curious fact that nicotine encourages the production of epinephrine or adrenaline in the body, and this acts as a muscle relaxant, which relieves the symptoms of asthma. Nicotine also inhibits the production of serotonin in the body, and serotonin is the 'baddie', related to histamine, which plays a major part in allergies.

At an international conference on environmental tobacco smoke (ETS, or 'passive smoking') at McGill University in 1989 (*not* a WHO conference), it was very cautiously suggested that:

> The possibility that the acute responses noted in some asthmatics result from a psychogenic [in the mind] reaction, as opposed to a physiologic [physical] response to ETS, needs to be investigated further. Psychological and emotional influences are known to be of considerable importance in asthmatic episodes .... It has been reported that suggestion may even affect pulmonary [lung] function in non-asthmatics ....

The question of ETS or 'passive smoking' and lung cancer is altogether more complicated, if only because so much more effort has been put into it by anti-smokers. It was touched off in 1981 by a study by Dr Hirayama in Japan, reported in the *British Medical*

Journal. He made use of a test devised by N. Mantel, who responded with an analysis of Hirayama's work that expressed doubts about its ambiguities and omissions, and also about the fact that Hirayama had confused statistical terms and made mistakes of up to 1,000% in another set of figures.

Hirayama replied that prominent statisticians, unnamed, had confirmed the validity of his test. This brought in J.R. Johnstone, a Fellow of the University of Western Australia, formerly Senior Research Fellow with Australia's Health and Medical Research Council, who commented on this reply of Hirayama's:

> In any other area of science – or indeed intellectual discourse generally – this would be enough to negate Hirayama's contribution.

Yet Hirayama's work has been used world-wide, and actually surfaced once again in 1997, quoted with apparently straight faces by the compilers of a report on heart disease and passive smoking.

In 1992 Dr Tage Voss, in his delightful *Smoking and Commonsense*, told us that an effective and acceptable way of cheering up boring scientific conferences is to have yet another go at Hirayama. He gives one example of such an attempt at light relief when someone pointed out that even if all Hirayama's arguments were taken literally, it could be shown that the conclusions he should have reached were exactly opposite to those he claimed.

Another pioneer in this field was Trichopolous in Greece. He found a slight risk, just barely statistically significant if you're not too fussy, for the non-smoking wives of smokers, but he also found that these non-smoking wives were more likely to get lung cancer than women who actually smoked themselves. Hirayama had found a similar anomaly.

This is very odd. Smokers are not only exposed to their own intake of smoke, but also to their own 'side-stream smoke', as it's called, from 'passive smoking'. If you accept these three studies, you must also accept that in these cases smoking has *protected* the 'victim' of 'passive smoking' from lung cancer.

Another study often quoted is that of Californian Seventh Day Adventists, who are forbidden to smoke on religious grounds. It is not unknown for people to do things they are forbidden to do on religious grounds. The study is based on very few cases, and a number of assumptions and calculations are made that are clearly incorrect, though the conclusions are irreproachably politically correct: 'passive smoking' is bad for you.

To sum up: of the thirty studies made by 1990, still quoted, six showed risk ratios that pointed to a danger, but were all statistically weak; that is, they would not have been taken seriously in an impartial judgment; and nine showed a risk ratio that pointed to a protective effect of passive smoking: that is, the passive smokers were in less danger. In these cases the risk ratios were as statistically weak as in the cases showing a danger, but if these latter were to be taken seriously, surely the others should be too. (Since then fourteen more studies have been recorded, but except for one that again shows a favourable result, that is, less risk for 'passive smokers', they have not altered the general picture.)

The Environmental Protection Agency

Then in 1992 the American Environmental Protection Agency (EPA) published an analysis of eleven selected studies on 'passive smoking', which was used to justify classifying ETS as a 'Group A: Known Human Carcinogen'.

To see what the EPA was up to, it should be remembered that in 1989 it had investigated diesel emissions, and produced a risk ratio for cancer of 2.6. These emissions were then classified as a 'Group B: Probable Human Carcinogen'. Another study on electro-magnetic fields found risk ratios of well over 3.0 (which any statistician would say suggested definitely significant risks). These were not even given a classification, nor were the well-recorded risks of keeping pet birds, with a risk ratio ranging from 2 to 6.7.

Yet the EPA study on passive smoking found a risk ratio of only 1.28. And this was only achieved by means of what one of the people employed by the agency described as 'fancy statistical footwork'. In brief, the EPA chose 11 of the more than 30 studies then known, and combined them into what is known as a meta-analysis. This consists of putting all the results from a number of studies together and stirring them about until you get something.

This can be justified only if all the studies in question have been run on much the same lines. But of course they haven't been. All researchers have different methods, which they are convinced are much better than anyone else's; they study different sets of people; they and their interviewers have different approaches, and some are more competent or scrupulous than others.

In this case, stir as it might, the EPA couldn't get the result it wanted. That's when more of the 'fancy statistical footwork' came into play. Risk ratios are calculated using what is technically known as the 95% confidence interval. This means that you have a 19 in 20 chance of being right. This is not the same as a certainty, as disappointed punters through the ages have found out, but for ordinary statistical purposes 95% is reckoned to be close enough.

It was not good enough for the EPA. They dropped the confidence interval to 90%, so giving themselves an increased chance of proving their case. With these rigged odds, they found just one of the eleven studies that produced a result. So on the basis of one study out of more than thirty, with a result achieved by fancy statistical footwork, they came out with their startling conclusions; conclusions that have been exploited around the world to justify more insidious attacks on individual freedoms.

Even in the US, even among government scientists, there have been protests against this misuse of science. The latest and most devastating assault was the recent federal court judgement (17 July 1998) that the EPA had totally failed to prove its central case that 'passive smoking' damaged the health of non-smokers. Judge Osteen riddled the EPA with a lethal volley of shot and shell: the EPA had failed to comply with 'procedural requirements set out by Congress'; it had changed its methodology to find a statistically significant association; rather than reach a conclusion *after* collecting information, researching and making findings, the EPA categorised ETS as a 'known cause of cancer' in 1989; its administrative record contains glaring deficiencies; the EPA began drafting a policy guide recommending workplace smoking bans *before* drafting the ETS Risk Assessment.

In short, the EPA report's conclusions have been shown to be quite unjustified. No wonder one US newspaper suggested that EPA should stand for Environmental Propaganda Agency!

Rotten science

People are already beginning to turn against orthodox science in many different ways, with 'alternative' this and that. The cults of pagan worship; the suburban witches who carry out weird rites in their sitting-rooms; the 'alternative' lifestyles of the New Age Travellers and the like; the innumerable 'alternative' medical treatments on offer; and perhaps saddest of all, the fact that the *Daily Telegraph* now offers an astrological column, all show a turning-away from what has been the great strength of Western civilization: the demand for reasonable proof and rational explanation for our beliefs.

This flight from reason can't simply be put down to human silliness. Orthodox science, i.e. knowledge, which is what 'science' means, has failed us time and again. If historians had seen to it that people were taught exactly what Druidism or witchcraft actually meant, and the origins and false basis of astrology, for instance, they wouldn't be so ready to make fools of themselves. If medicine had bothered to investigate the claims of 'alternative' treatments, and had helped us sort out those that really do some good, we wouldn't be at the mercy of so many fast-talking quacks.

Now science is failing us again on this question of smoking. The message it is giving to those of us who have not already been brain-washed is that 'experts' think we will swallow any old nonsense as long as it's tricked out with a lot of long words and worrying-sounding statistics. Remember the hysteria about AIDs which was to rampage through the general public?

A former Canadian Health Minister, Marc Lalonde, put it very plainly in an influential 1974 report:

> Science is full of 'ifs', 'buts', and 'maybes', while messages designed to influence the public must be loud, clear, and unequivocal .... The scientific 'yes, but' is essential to research, but for modifying human behaviour of the population it sometimes produces the 'uncertain sound'. This is all the excuse needed by many to cultivate and tolerate an environment and lifestyle that is hazardous to health.

Or, as an understandably anonymous academic acquaintance of

the Yale University epidemiologist whom we've met before, Professor Alvan Feinstein, said, on the EPA report:

> Yes, it's rotten science, but it's in a worthy cause. It will help us to get rid of cigarettes and become a smoke-free society.

The message, then, is: 'We're justified in lying to you because it's good for you, you poor idiots.' Goebbels couldn't have put it better, with his recommendation of 'the big lie'. Is it any wonder, then, that a fear is growing that science will so discredit itself that the 'alternatives' will take over? After all, genuine science pretty often turns out to be right eventually, if you keep a wary eye on it. Homeopathy and aromatherapy couldn't have dealt with malaria and cholera, and modern surgery can do much, if it sometimes tries to do too much. No one has ever been able to show that those who run their lives according to the readings of astrology are more successful than those who don't; astronomy has enormously increased our knowledge of the universe, and if rightly used, should increase that of ourselves.

All the Druids' predictions based on the flight of birds and the writhings of sacrificed victims did not help them against the Romans, and for all the earnest practice of witches like Gilles de Rais, who killed several hundred children in his attempts to raise the devil, the devil never came.

But if nannying scientists are going to treat us like stupid children whose lives have to be 'modified', and are prepared to use lies and 'rotten science' to do so, we are going to lose all respect for them, and with it lose trust in real science, together with the rotten sort. Let us hope that heaven will protect the environment, since it seems, on its present form, that the Environmental Protection Agency is not likely to make a very good job of it.

Dear little kiddies

It can be taken for granted, human nature being what it is, that as contraception becomes an essential part of our lifestyle, abortion the new morality, and crimes against (and by) children grow, sentimentality about them grows accordingly. It was perhaps inevitable that the effects, or reputed effects, of passive smoking on children would soon be exploited.

P. Cameron in 1967 published a paper, quoted in the report of the McGill conference mentioned earlier, entitled: 'The Presence of Pets and Smoking as Correlates of Perceived Disease', thereby succeeding in attacking two human pleasures at once. After that the studies came thick and fast, fifty or more of them up to 1990.

There have been no very startling results, though we are told cautiously that there does seem to be a correlation between parental smoking and respiratory disease in young children, which decreases markedly as the children get older. Remember that coincidence is not causation. There are other explanations, including one which is very unpopular with the authorities, which is disguised by the words 'socioeconomically disadvantaged' (in plain speech, poor). It is a well-established fact that smoking is much more common among the poor. It's about the only pleasure that many of them can afford. There is also the wartime mentality described above: their lives are hard: smoking gives them that little release from tension, the feeling that they have at their command a little pleasure, that while they light their cigarettes and settle down to enjoy them they are in control of their own lives. Those who never need to call up such feelings have no idea of how much they mean. There is also the unquestioned fact that children inherit or catch disease from their parents, and those who are handicapped by chronic or often-repeated illnesses are likely to be less able to compete successfully in the job market. Those who do manage to do so are to be respected, but there are some whose health problems, combined perhaps with other factors, are too much for them. Their children are likely to be disadvantaged, whether anyone in the household smokes or not.

The American Surgeon General's 1979 report noted that parental smoking was associated with increased respiratory illness in children, but also with increased hospitalisations of infants because of injuries and poisonings. The report suggested that this points to parental neglect rather than parental smoking. It would be more charitable to say that parents dogged by ill-health and poverty may be less able to give their children the wished-for care.

One study showed a marked difference between children living in an industrial area and those in a rural area, but in general poverty was what showed up most clearly as the cause of children's illnesses. This is never likely to be popular among health experts, who are pretty sure to be government employees of one sort or another. Few of us care to quarrel with our bread and butter, and governments of all complexions do not like to be reminded of these intractable problems. Far better to blame it all on smoking, and continue to draw your salary.

How to find words for cruelty like this?

But these shenanigans pale before those of the affair of SIDS (Sudden Infant Death Syndrome, or cot death). The plain truth seems to be that no one really knows what causes cot deaths. *Black's Medical Dictionary*, 1990, listed the following possible causes: smothering by a soft pillow, a virus infection, an innate tendency to poor breathing control and likelihood to stop breathing if the infant has a cold, an allergy to milk, being bottle-fed, being deficient in Vitamin E, suffering from the spontaneous production of botulinum toxin in the gut.

Other causes suggested by various authorities have included under-developed kidneys, too low birth weight, scarring of the brain tissue, meningitis, brain defects, bacteria in the nose and throat, synthetic bedding, infections conveyed in the bedding, toxic gases given off by the bedding, over-heating, wrapping the baby up too tightly, vaccination against whooping cough, sharing a bed with the baby if you're in the habit of drinking a lot. No wonder that Dr Sydney Segal of Vancouver told the *Winnipeg Free Press* on 2 February 1992:

> There isn't any prime cause. SIDS is just where a child dies suddenly for no cause that we know.

Webster's Medical Dictionary merely restates the ignorance:

> deaths due to unknown causes of an infant in apparently good health.

So it seemed logical to those people to whom this sort of thing seems logical to blame smoking. The Royal College of Physicians stated, in *Smoking and the Young* (30 June 1993) that 365 infant deaths a year have been 'associated' with maternal smoking. This 365 represented approximately 27% of the then total of 1,326 cot deaths a year.

But according to the official figures 29% of the women in this country smoked, and the total was likely to be higher among women of child-bearing age because smoking is more usual among the young. In fact the figure quoted would appear to show that a slightly higher proportion of cot deaths occurred in the babies of non-smoking mothers.

In any case, one factor has now been proved beyond any doubt to be a cause of cot death. It is not the only cause, because there are still such deaths, though very many fewer, since mothers were advised to put babies to sleep on their backs instead of their stomachs. A very well-publicised media campaign was mounted to see that this was done. Why did they ever put their babies to sleep on their stomachs in the first place? It is not the natural position that the babies will take up once they can arrange themselves as they like in bed. It is not, surely, the position that inexperienced young mothers would think of putting the baby into. It is not the position that seems to be shown in all the pictures and photographs of sleeping infants. It is certainly not what their mothers or grand-mothers did.

It was used because experts decided it was a good idea. On 30 March 1993, the medical correspondent of the *Daily Telegraph* wrote:

> Twenty years ago baby experts at an international meeting in the Netherlands concluded that premature babies thrived best when put to sleep on their fronts. Like bushfire, the fashionable message spread that all babies were safest in this sleeping position even though the studies were on premature babies only .... But through the 1970s and 1980s most doctors and midwives rigidly advised sleeping on the front. 'It would have been heresy not to,' said one.

During the twenty years that this advice was given, cot deaths ran at some 1,500 a year. After the campaign against it, the deaths dropped by 60%. In those twenty years, can it be that the experts were responsible for more than 15,000 deaths?

As soon as the advice had become general, voices had been raised against it. Dr Susan Beal, an Australian paediatrician, tried for eleven years to persuade her colleagues that it was the medical advice that was responsible for the rise in cot deaths. Eventually a question was included in a survey into cot death that was being carried out in the Avon district. The answers were such that it was thought that they must be a 'statistical aberration', and publication was held up for a year. When the figures were at last released, and the campaign to put babies to sleep on their backs got under way, the deaths dropped by 60%, as noted.

The results were extraordinarily convincing. An interesting fact also emerged: Asian and Chinese mothers had a lower rate of these deaths from the beginning, because they did what their mothers, not the doctors and midwives, told them.

Gulp!

So this deadly advice had killed more than fifteen thousand babies. You would expect that someone would say: 'Sorry!' or at least: 'Gulp!' Not a bit of it. Dead silence, and a further attack on smoking mothers.

When, shortly afterwards, a considerable amount of evidence was brought forward to show that another factor in these deaths was mattresses treated with fireproof materials, there was another extraordinarily violent attack on this idea. Could it have been that those who led the attack knew all too well that it would be easy to connect the fact that putting babies to sleep on their stomachs would bring their faces into direct contact with these mattresses, and so add to the dangers of the prone position? And who had advised them to put the babies to sleep in this position? It seems they did not want to be reminded of this.

Christopher Booker pointed out in the *Sunday Telegraph* (28 July 1996) that the cot death rate started to drop in the late 1980s, when manufacturers began to phase out the use of these chemicals. As Booker says, in the 1940s, when over 80% of the population smoked, cot deaths were almost unknown. The *Lancet* (18 March 1995) has a brief account of the information collected by the national Confidential Enquiry into Stillbirths and Deaths in Infancy (CESDDI). In the final paragraph it is stated that:

Further multivariate analysis showed that neither the sex of the infant nor maternal smoking had any significant effect on the odds ratio given in the table.

Professor Fleming, who had carried out research into the causes of cot death, said in a broadcast on BBC Radio 1 on 9 September 1994:

> what sets off that process is unclear. I think that almost certainly there's not one single cause ....

Yet the 'smoking causes cot deaths' legend persists. Endless items in the media giving professional advice to pregnant women tell them again and again not to smoke because it will kill their babies. Parents who have lost a baby are devastated with guilt, to the point, in some cases, of being suicidal.

The cult of 'blame the victim' causes endless suffering to patients and their families. In cases like this, when the families are already racked with guilt, and the doctors must know what a burden of guilt they themselves bear for the past, it is almost impossible to believe that they can indulge in such cruelty.

This brief review of the myth of 'passive smoking' (recently further shown up by an article in the *Sunday Telegraph* on a World Health Organisation report that has not been published), shows the burden of guilt borne by the EPA and others who continue to spread the myth.

Guilt for spreading fear, for creating enmity between non-smokers and smokers, who seldom in the past felt any need for this kind of ugly malevolence; guilt, in an age already sufficiently disturbed by bad manners and oafishness, for giving further reasons for the display of such behaviour.

Perhaps, to be charitable, it arises more from stupidity, ignorance, gullibility, than from deliberate cruelty. This was brought home to me by the experience of trying to convince a prominent medical man that he was causing great distress to parents who had lost a baby by insisting that it was their own fault for smoking. The expression on the hot red face said more plainly than any words: 'Are you trying to tell me that patients have *feelings*?'

6

Hate the sin – and the sinner

We are all so very nice nowadays. Political correctness is very nice, almost to the point of being dainty. We can't talk about people being disabled, only 'differently abled'. The blind aren't blind, and the old aren't old, and the disabled aren't disabled: they're all something else that sounds better, at least to the people using the euphemisms. Whether this makes the blind or the old or the disabled feel better in any way never seems to be discussed. After all, they know when they are blind or old or disabled, and they know the very real problems they face. It's difficult to see how these problems are in any way ameliorated by words.

But these prettinesses seem to make the people using the terms feel better, though they are very likely the sort of people who would pride themselves on using the plainest possible words for bodily functions, and would laugh at the Victorians for talking about 'being in the family way' instead of pregnant. Perhaps every age feels the need of something to be dainty about.

So we, at least in the West, have to be very, very nice in so many ways. We can't say anything that could in the vaguest way be thought to be deleterious about different races any more – except of course white, Christian, educated American or English men who are fair game – you have to be careful about their female compatriots, because you might get the feminists after you.

Nor must you be unkind, or even slightly less than thoroughly supportive, about anyone's sexual preferences. Nor can you be safe in saying anything about religions, or in suggesting that there's the least difference between any of them, except of course for the one professed by someone who might well shoot you if you don't admit that his is much the best.

So much niceness is bound to upset many human beings. Many

of us define ourselves by our hatreds. We could say instead of 'I think, therefore I am,' 'I hate, therefore I am.' Hating may well be something that many people can do better than thinking. A hate object is necessary for these people. And who better than the smoker? He or she is visible. You can't have a real hate object you can't identify. You must be able to abuse him or her on sight.

It still surprises many smokers, even after all these years of being hate objects, to find how appallingly rude otherwise inoffensive people can be about smoking and smokers.

What do you say to the man or woman who tells you that smoking is a 'filthy habit'? You may be tempted to say that to eat or drink as much as they plainly do, or something of the sort, is perhaps just as filthy, or filthier. But of course you don't. One of the curious things about smokers is that they seldom answer back.

The Christian spirit

There is a tea-room attached to a very beautiful and much-visited church in Oxfordshire that has a notice in the window: 'Smokers most unwelcome and evicted immediately.' The *Oxford English Dictionary* defines 'evict' as follows: 'expel (person); recover by legal process.' How are they proposing to evict the smoker? Is there a muscular curate on call who will charge out of the back room and evict the offender by wielding the bishop's crook, borrowed for the purpose? Or have the good ladies running the tea-room, none of them exactly in the first flush of youth, been learning karate? As for the legal process, have they a learned attorney as well as the curate in the back room?

It is easy to make fun of such silliness, but it can make people feel very uncomfortable and truly hurt, which indeed seems to be its aim. There is some real hatred behind it, and an English country church should surely be the wrong place for it. Yet no one seems to have dared to point this out, or that a simple notice such as 'Thank you for not smoking' is always honoured. Whoever put that notice up wanted to hurt, and no doubt is very pleased with the result.

The simple desire to hurt should never be ignored. Many very politically correct people show it clearly in the savagery with which they go for their hate object.

The caring profession

There is no lack of doctors who will proudly turn smoking patients off their lists. Smokers have been refused operations, and one at least, Harry Elphick, has died as a result. A man severely injured in an accident, which surely could not have been caused by his smoking, was refused treatment because he smoked.

In the *Daily Telegraph* (21 March 1993), a bewildered man interviewed in a pub said:

> I just went to hospital because I'd broken my thumb. The first thing they asked me was how much I drank and whether I smoked.

In 1992 doctors in Kent were told, by Kent's Family Health Services Authority, to record patients' smoking habits and compile a 'hit-list'.

Doctors have been instructed to give advice to patients on smoking, and are actually paid for doing so. Surgery, as reported in an article in *Heart* (1996), has been less likely to be offered to smokers, and the surgeons used the threat of refusing surgery to blackmail patients into giving up smoking.

The cruelty implied in this seems almost unbelievable, especially since there is some evidence that in some cases smokers actually do better after heart surgery. (There is evidence in a well-known study, the International Tissue Plasminogen Activator/Streptokinase Mortality Trial, which surgeons must be aware of.) The only reason for their behaviour is plain cruelty. Take a very sick man or woman (they must be so to qualify for heart surgery), and bully them into giving up what may be their only pleasure and consolation, and refuse them treatment if they won't.

This cruelty could be seen in the case of a woman who was told that if her husband had only given up smoking four years before instead of two years, he wouldn't have got lung cancer. Nothing about 'estimated', 'not be unreasonable to attribute', 'assumed', 'may well be', or any other of the vague phrases seen above. And nothing of course about the Australian or French studies, or the lifestyle studies, or the cancer cases that weren't found in postmortems; just the flat statement that filled the woman with guilt because she had not persuaded her husband to give up smoking four years instead of two years before.

In any case, lung cancer is very seldom diagnosed, correctly or not, before the patient is in his or her late fifties, and most people have started smoking in their teens. It is generally recognised that it takes many years to develop. It seems almost unbelievable that in the face of these facts the doctor could make this flat statement. It certainly made the woman, and presumably also her husband for what was left of his life, very miserable.

But this cruelty fades beside that of the doctors who continued to blame women for the cot deaths of their babies even after it had been proved that most of these were caused by medical advice to put them to sleep on their stomachs.

However, among the patients refused heart surgery there was one who got his operation because it was paid for by a cigarette company: there seemed no objection to a paying smoker. There is something heartening in that: the true fanatic can't be bought.

But those who can be bought can see the advantages of having fanatics to break the ground for them. Once the fanatic has preached so persuasively that the general public has been brainwashed into thinking there is some great danger that must be tackled, those whose main interest in life is making money can move in and cash in.

Top of these are of course governments and lawyers. Governments are always looking for ways of increasing taxes. Tobacco is easy to tax. And lawyers, especially in the US, are always looking for someone to sue.

A splendid recent example is the way in which tobacco companies in the US were persuaded to make an agreement to pay $365 billion in a settlement. This money was to go to the governments of the states involved, in return for a promise not to prosecute, and of course to the lawyers. Nothing was allocated to any private citizens. And even this was said to be not enough, if more could be wrung out of the companies. No agreement has been signed, not surprisingly. At least the Danish pirates paid off by Ethelred the Unready with his famous 'Danegeld' went away once they'd got the money, and waited a bit before coming back.

But the American anti-smokers announce that their intention is to ruin the tobacco industry. They have the proud example of the anti-drinking forces that with prohibition ruined most of the country's brewing industry (some say all). That didn't stop the Americans drinking because the bootleggers were ready. Organised crime received a colossal boost, from the repercussions of which the Americans are still suffering. Some of the saner people in the anti-smoker game do point this out uneasily from time to time, but there is no arguing with the fanatics.

What makes a fanatic? It's tempting to say stupidity, and with many that is plainly the main characteristic. Ignoring all the evidence, all that common-sense tells them, all the experience of the ages, comes easily to some people. They know, and that is enough. Useless to tell them of the evidence, to show them figures, to point out contradictions. Save your breath.

Holier than thou

There is also a strong puritanical streak in many people, especially in the USA. It seems that they have rejected all that made the Puritans great: their courage, their faith, their resourcefulness, and retained only their least attractive feature, that hatred of pleasure, so well described by the great humorist H.L. Mencken, who called it: 'The haunting fear that someone, somewhere, is happy.'

There are said to be people who suffer from a psychological condition that makes them incapable of enjoying anything. They are much to be pitied, except that because of their utter lack of understanding of what it is to enjoy anything they can't understand other people who are not so handicapped, and so make their lives as unpleasant as only a complete lack of fellow-feeling can. Their ideal appears to be a life grimly devoted to preserving health. In the past it was equally grimly devoted to getting to Heaven, though they certainly wouldn't have enjoyed that if they'd succeeded. It would have been too full of people they'd disapproved of in life.

Just as the earlier Puritans were heaven-bent and determined to see that others got there too, even if it meant that their lives on earth were hell, so this ideal of perfect health is to be imposed on others, even if this means that all their everyday pleasures are snatched away from them.

Yet the life-style studies mentioned above show that this doesn't have the healthy effect hoped for. The Finnish businessmen who cut their smoking and drinking, ate healthy food, and took exercise and drugs for their heart conditions, were considerably worse off than those who did none of these things. Exercise is fine if you take it because you enjoy it. But the sight of thinly clad joggers shivering or sweating, pounding hard pavements with grisly determination, suggests anything but enjoyment. Did you ever see a jogger smiling?

Very few modern drugs are without side-effects, many worse than the original disease. They're certainly not enjoyable to take. Healthy food, or what is declared to be such by health enthusiasts, is nasty. Sugar is nice. So are cream, butter, real milk with the cream left on, meat with enough fat left on it to flavour it and make it cook properly, chocolate, bread and beef dripping, and vegetables cooked with salt and with butter on.

On the salt question, it is now said that it is only people with high blood pressure who need to cut down on it. And cholesterol, once declared an enemy of the human race almost on a level with smoking, is now being found to be a necessity. Drink, used reasonably, is nice. Some is now being declared to be good for you, notably red wine. Much red wine on the market is poor stuff, no particular pleasure to drink, which may have something to do with why it is now allowed.

Garlic should be consumed in huge quantities. Since it has the peculiar property of stunning the taste-buds, if you eat the amount recommended you won't be able to taste it (or anything else), so you won't enjoy it. And the people sitting next to you will hate it.

So we see the Puritan principle in action again: eat nothing that you like, and as in the past that eased your way to salvation, it will now put you on the road to health and long life. Since most people now have no faith in a future life, all they can hope for is as long a life as possible on this earth.

Those whom the gods love die young

Have they never seen a geriatric ward? Doctors, most of whom have, when asked how they would prefer to die all chose a quick death, either from a heart attack or a head injury or a quick fatal accident.

It's not much of a life that is entirely spent in warding off death. It isn't even a very successful one. As previously pointed out, the Greeks, smoking more cigarettes than anyone else in the world, drinking plenty, and not noticeably addicted to jogging, have a higher life-expectancy than the health-conscious, earnestly jogging, non-smoking, and the rest of it, Americans. Apart from this, it might be said that every day or hour or minute spent worrying about your health is lost from your life.

Some worries we must have: the constructive ones, which lead us to do something positive to improve our lives. But the sort of futile worry that leads us from one fancy diet to another, one gym or exercise centre to another, one health guru to (alas!) a dozen others, is so much waste of time. Your age of death is to a very great extent determined by outside factors: viruses that you can pick up unknowingly however cleanly you live, the accident that you could have done nothing to prevent, the madman who happens to come your way with a weapon, or is in charge of your country or a neighbouring country and decides to make war, the doctor who makes a wrong diagnosis. And by the length of your parents' lives – all the evidence is that there is a very strong hereditary element in longevity – and above all by where you chance to have been born. If it was Cambodia a healthy diet would have done nothing for you, and there are many other places where it wouldn't help much, even if it was available there.

A survey was carried out by the former Distressed Gentlefolk's Aid Association, now the DGAA Homelife, on one hundred centenarians. The delightful report on it did not, unfortunately, give precise figures, but was none the less admirable for the sympathy and understanding with which the survey had obviously been carried out. It showed that what was common to almost all was a positive, outgoing attitude to life, hard work continuing well past the usual retirement age (two were still working), and eating a good traditional diet; that is, one that must have included most of the foods now declared to be bad for you. Many had smoked and drunk, and some still did.

There used to be a cheerfully gloomy saying: 'Well, when your number's up, it's up.' Does it really help you to forget these bits of aged folk wisdom? After all, the people who guided their lives by them were going by all the experience of the past. Even if it can't be proved to be true, it is surely a healthier and happier attitude than that of the extremists who spend so much time arranging for a long life in the future that they fail to enjoy the present.

But you can't get away from extremists. Sometimes it seems that they can't rest until they've made everyone else as miserable as they are themselves. That is another very important element in the characters of the fanatics. They are people who are deeply troubled by anyone who differs from them in any way. Another cheerful bit of folklore: 'Live and let live,' infuriates them. Perhaps because they are not really living in any positive and enjoyable sense, they can't bear to see other people looking as if they are.

Of course they will never admit to this. Their motive is always to save others from themselves. The misery they inflict on them for the moment is to save them much greater misery in the future. The trouble with all such noble aims is that the present misery is real and tangible: the future is always uncertain. If we all gave up smoking, eating 'unhealthy' food, and enjoying ourselves in politically incorrect ways, we could still die of any of the causes given on the previous page.

And if it's good for you?

The outpouring of hate against tobacco, whipped up by politicians and the media, one suspects, when they want to divert attention from something else, is a tragedy not only because the lives of so many inoffensive people are being made miserable by it, but also because there is some very real evidence to show that tobacco has certain definite benefits.

Dr Tage Voss describes some of these. Smokers, he says, have a lower rate of intestinal cancer, Parkinson's Disease, trigeminal neuralgia, tumours in the central nervous system, and diabetes. These are all unpleasant complaints, mostly lasting a long time and causing great trouble and misery to all concerned. An article in the *British Medical Bulletin* (1996) describes the 'Beneficial Effects of Nicotine and Cigarette Smoking: the Real, the Possible and the Spurious'.

Smoking women have lower rates of fibroids in the womb, and of endometriosis, which produces extremely painful menstruation.

Endometrial cancer (cancer of the womb) is definitely less frequent in smokers. Smoking in pregnancy reduces the risk of hypertensive disorders and eclampsia, which are both dangerous. It also reduces vomiting.

Smokers do not suffer so much from mouth ulcers, and decidedly less from ulcerative colitis, a revolting complaint. One study showed that they suffered less from bad acne. The article also refers to the definite positive effect on Parkinson's, and also that weird condition, Tourette's Syndrome, sufferers from which can find themselves involuntarily shouting and swearing. As everyone knows, smoking is also useful in controlling body weight. With obesity becoming a major health problem, especially in the US, and food already under attack from the puritans and health fascists, victims might like to decide what they would prefer to be persecuted for.

But the greatest benefit of all is in Alzheimer's Disease. This is the most dreadful fate that can befall anyone. The sufferers gradually lose everything that makes them human beings, and take on Shakespeare's 'mere oblivion ... sans everything'.

It is a very common disease in this country and others. Dr David Weeks, of the Royal Edinburgh Hospital, said in the *Daily Telegraph* (7 March 1989):

> The Alzheimer's Disease epidemic of the 21st century is going to be
> considerably more significant than the AIDS epidemic will be. It is
> a dreadful disease for sufferers, and for their relatives and friends.

He should know: the same article tells us that of the 1,000 beds at the hospital, 600 are occupied by Alzheimer's victims. Four years ago the Alzheimer's Disease Society said there were about 600,000 people with dementia in the UK, and about 70% of these have Alzheimer's.

It is a specific disease, with easily identified effects on the brain, and it can be hereditary. It destroys neurons in the brain, and once destroyed these can never be replaced. The only known method of prevention is smoking. In *The Times* (7 September 1993), Dr James Le Fanu wrote:

Smokers have a 50% reduced risk of developing Alzheimer's – and the more smoked the greater the protection.

The article ends by saying that doctors should encourage people over 60 to take up smoking.

The *New Scientist* (9 October 1993) discussed this research, and added that much of it had been held up because of the violence of the feeling about smokers.

Elaine Perry, of the MRC Neurochemical Pathology Unit at New General Hospital, said that drug companies had been 'rather slow' to explore the value of nicotinic receptors in Alzheimer's Disease. They have little interest in letting researchers investigate the activity of nicotine analogues in the brain. Yet, she adds, if you administer nicotine to a damaged animal brain, it recovers much faster.

This backs up the notion that nicotine prevents the degeneration in Alzheimer's disease.

This points up the well-known fact that smoking improves mental performance. The article in the *British Medical Bulletin*, mentioned above, lists:

modest improvements in vigilance and information processing, facilitation of some motor responses, and perhaps enhancement of memory.

It couldn't be more ungraciously admitted, but it has been confirmed in numerous other works.

As for Parkinson's Disease, Karl Olov Gagerstrom, of the Swedish drugs company Kabi Pharmacia, says:

When I speak to neurologists handling Parkinson's patients about nicotine they cannot believe it. They cannot imagine prescribing what to them is such a dirty drug.

So patients and their families enduring the agony of Parkinson's are denied the only known alleviation because the anti-smokers would carry on if anyone suggested it.

The article adds another disease to the list of those benefited by smoking: rheumatoid arthritis. This too is agonising, and very common.

Perhaps it's worth while pointing out that nicotine is the only enjoyable substance that has a favourable effect on the brain. Alcohol certainly hasn't, nor have any of the drugs with which the anti-smokers compare tobacco. Even the mildest, cannabis, produces paranoid symptoms in some 30% of users. There's quite enough paranoia around in the normal course of events without adding 30% more.

The anti-smokers have tried to avoid these unwelcome conclusions by saying that smokers don't live long enough to get any of these diseases. Apart from the fact that many of them, diabetes in particular, can start in extreme youth or in middle age, what about the Greeks, the Japanese, the Swiss? With higher smoking rates than us and the Americans and longer life expectancies, surely they live long enough to get anything that's going.

The hate object

But there is no arguing with these people. If you want to know exactly what moves them, perhaps it would help to look again at the statement, quoted earlier, by Professor Glantz.

> The main thing the science has done on the issue of ETS [environmental tobacco smoke], in addition to help people like me to pay mortgages, is it has legitimised the concerns that people have that they don't like cigarette smoke. And that is a strong emotional force that needs to be harnessed and used. We're on a roll, and the bastards are on the run.

This seems to include everything that can be seen to move the anti-smokers. First of all, there is money in it: government money for schemes and research that pay the people working on them well, and 'compensation' extracted from the tobacco companies; then there are the sensitivities of those people who 'don't like cigarette smoke', and think that that is enough to let loose a full-blown persecution; the emotionalism that must be 'harnessed' and 'used' so that, as Professor Glantz himself says, his mortgage can be paid, and the people who don't like cigarette smoke can make a crusade of their priggishness. Above all, there is the sheer sense of power: 'We're on a roll, the bastards are on the run.'

In what other occupation could such people get such a buzz? Where else could they feel at liberty to insult so many people? The anti-smokers boast that they have made smokers outcasts, pariahs, 'socially unacceptable'. What fun for the sort of people who find that sort of thing fun. The whole history of human persecution shows that there are always people who need to feel 'in' by making other people feel 'out'. If the anti-smokers were sincere about their desire to make us all healthier they would not carefully ignore all the evidence that shows that health does not result from such deprivations, still less would they fabricate evidence to show that it does.

They want a hate object, and the smoker is it. We can console ourselves by thinking that if it wasn't us, it would be somebody else perhaps less able to cope, so we're doing a public service. And we can always light up our cigarette or cigar or pipe, and relax, and *they can't*.

Part II

The truth will out

Does smoking really kill anybody?

With a pipe never far from my mouth, I have learned that some non-smokers, especially ladies, profess to enjoy the smell of to-bacco, while others, especially sad ex-smokers, are less enthusiastic. But if smokers exercise normal consideration and courtesy, few ordinary people in my long experience get unduly worked up on the issue.

£1,000 a smoke?

A useful litmus test I have found is the story of a pair of notices plastered all over the buses in Barnet where I live, one the familiar, ubiquitous NO SMOKING and the other warning against travelling without a ticket. When I tell people that the advertised fine for fare-dodgers is £5, and invite them to guess what a naughty smoker might have to stump up, most answers fall between £10 and £50 with a very occasional £100. I have yet to meet anyone who is not astonished to be told that the fine threatened for smoking, even upstairs on the double-deckers of these now privatised buses, is a 'maximum £1,000'. The most apt quip I've heard is: 'Why not a million?' This informal attitude survey over many months suggests that most normal citizens do not see smoking as ranking with the great evils of the day such as, say, mugging, drugs, divorce – or perhaps election promises. No one sees it as 200 times more culpable than cheating a bus company of the fare. Yet for a militant minority and their captive politi-cians, stubbing out cigarettes seems to loom larger than – dare I say – whether Britain should be 'stubbed out' in a United States of Europe!

Within a fortnight of the General Election in May 1997, Tony

Blair announced the dawn of a New Labour era and the press made great play of the spin-doctors' boast that all the new ministers had 'hit the ground running', though later performance suggested some had landed on their heads. The new Prime Minister duly acknowledged the daunting task of putting right 18 years of 'Tory damage'. Yet in his very first speech to the Commons after the election, he found time to warn smokers that they would be at the forefront of the crusade – starting with a White Paper on the burning issue of banning tobacco advertising. It struck me at the time rather like Churchill in 1940 rallying the people to brace themselves for tears, toil and sweat – and then announcing a national drive to keep Britain tidy.

Of course, Mr Blair hadn't had the benefit of Judith Hatton's lethal analysis of the propaganda against smoking, especially the will o' the wisp 'passive' variety, and he probably felt a glow of innocent pride as he declared his personal commitment to this great crusade. Yet the only memory most of the public have on the subject is probably the imbroglio into which he stumbled over the promise of a comprehensive ban on sports sponsorship by tobacco companies – with the special exception of Labour's Bernie Ecclestone and his Formula One motor racing.

A confidence trick

Although significant as showing the practical difficulties and economic costs of trying to implement simple anti-smoking slogans, the declaration of war against tobacco raises a far deeper issue. The headlines about New Labour's historic landslide victory obscured the sobering truth that they had polled fewer votes in the election than the now devastated Tories had done only five years earlier. Indeed, closer inspection of the figures revealed a remarkable fact. Although Labour could lay impressive claim to support by as many as 43% of voters, only 71% of the electorate had bothered to vote so their true tally was a mere 30.8% of the electorate. But, wait a minute: this was rather less than the despised one-third or so of the adult population who, despite all the battering of scare stories, intimidation and higher taxes, continue to smoke. Behold, no sooner had the people's ballots been counted than we were treated to the Roman spec-

tacle of 33% of the plebs bracing themselves for further chastisement to be jubilantly administered in the name of less than 31%!
The further fact that Labour supporters are drawn disproportion-
ately from socio-economic classes C2/DE, who smoke more than
A/Bs, suggests that self-flagellation is now to be added to the other
punishments of smokers.

Here we glimpse the unsuspected confidence trick which is daily
perpetrated in the guise of universal democracy. After a working
lifetime spent studying the shaping – and more often mis-shaping
– of public policy, I have come to see the war on smokers as no
more than a symptom of a more general malaise, namely the
almost indiscriminate *politicisation* of everyday life discernible in
advanced democratic societies. All politicians become addicted to
it, but none more than socialists of all parties who set no limits to
their itch to interfere. With the single, possibly tenuous, exception
of Switzerland – whose prime minister, if they have one, is
completely unknown outside the 26 largely self-governing can-
tons – ruling politicians have everywhere come to arrogate to
themselves a pervasive, high-profile, self-important role as the
solvers of all society's problems. And what if most of us don't
have problems, at least not of a kind we wish to delegate to such
people? Then, politicians are easy prey to the ready panaceas of
single-issue pressure groups whose shrill, concentrated, orches-
trated demands swamp the mostly moderate opinions of the
dispersed majority.

Throughout the present century, and especially since the dawn
of democratic socialism in 1945, we can trace the accelerated
degeneration of government from being the guardian of hard-won
individual liberties to becoming the instrument of organised special
interest groups seeking favours at the expense of the unorganised
majority. As a result, the classical liberal conception of limited
government under a stable rule of law has been swamped by the
almost indiscriminate invasion of personal freedom from the almost casual multiplication of statutes. From being the servants of
the people, politicians have increasingly become their masters in a
morass of unlimited government.

Yet, if politicians are acting on behalf of the sovereign voter, it
may be asked: why should any limit be set to their arbitary power
to grant or withhold favours in return for the votes of their constitu-

ents? When Mr Blair starts talking of a crusade against tobacco advertising, the humble question 'to smoke or not to smoke' would seem to raise rather large issues of political, even constitutional, principle that go far beyond the hobbling of press freedom.

We can scorn the presumption of puny politicians. We can try to shame them by mocking their self-righteous pose as servants of the 'public interest'. We can remind them of Adam Smith's definition of

> that insidious and crafty animal, vulgarly called a statesman or politician, whose councils are directed by the momentary fluctuations of affairs.

(And, remember, that was in 1776, before politicians turned professional!)

In his own interest, the politician with an itch to interfere should heed Smith's prescient warning – before the days of tabloid papers – that he will only 'load himself with a most unnecessary attention'. We might even turn a little nasty and hint that political activism has less to do with helping others than with the perennial search for votes as the non-royal route to their ultimate goal – power, position, and the accompanying perks. Of course, politicians of every conceivable stripe subscribe to a single legend, namely that power is sought only to 'do good in the public interest'. But it's their choice of 'good', while the power they seek is to bend us – the sovereign people – to their purposes. Unconscious of the implied contempt, they 'treat other people's lives as the proper product of their own activity'. Whether from the right or the left, however well intentioned, paternalism ends up treating adults like children.

But what if the paternalist justifies discrimination against smokers on the ground that they are damaging their own health?

How much risk?

The most cogent counter-argument is that there are many risky activities adults choose to indulge in – motoring, drinking, hanggliding, sailing, ski-ing, horse riding, walking out at night, even getting married – without incurring the further risk of official chastisement. It is not only in financial investment that people's inclination or aversion to risk varies widely. It is perhaps understandable that many older people appear concerned with nothing more than staying alive but, in the words of an unusually wise academic philosopher, Kenneth Minogue: '... a civilisation dominated by such an imperative would not survive too long.'

Another shrewd academic, this time a professor of psychology, David Warburton, has said: 'The single-minded pursuit of health is a symptom of ill-health, hypochondria,' overdoing it perhaps by adding a quotation from Plato: 'Attention to health is the greatest hindrance to life.'

A second counter-argument, elaborated by Judith Hatton, is that the health risks of smoking to the smoker are grossly exaggerated. Leaving aside the question-begging health warnings on every packet of cigarettes and tobacco, the scare-mongering by ASH and the Health Education Authority go well beyond consumer education. They should carry a 'truth warning' against government-financed 'information'.

A vivid example of exaggeration was provided by a robust, independent Australian Professor of mathematical statistics, Peter Finch, in an instructive paper republished by FOREST as 'Lies, Damned Lies ...'. He took the official statistics of annual mortality and contrasted them with the warning that younger smokers (under 45) suffer 15 times the risk of non-smokers of dying of coronary heart disease. It is nicely calculated to bolster the message that SMOKING KILLS. But is it an informative way of presenting a difference in annual risk – on the showing of the anti-smoking lobby themselves – between *7 per 100,000* for non-smokers and *104 per 100,000* for smokers? True, 104 is roughly 15 times 7. But Professor Finch obligingly re-works the same figures to show that a smoker has 99.9% of the annual chance of the non-smoker of *escaping death from a coronary.* The trick to grasp is that a large increase on a tiny risk may still remain a small risk.

Turning to lung cancer, Professor Finch quotes the standard Doll & Hill figures as showing that heavy smokers face almost 24 times the annual risk faced by non-smokers of dying from that disease. This time the increase is from 7 per 100,000 to 166 per 100,000, which still leaves the smoker with 99.8% of the annual chance enjoyed by non-smokers of *escaping* death from lung cancer.

Shifting from annual risks to life-time risks for the general population, it has been estimated that around 1 in 3 will suffer some form of cancer during their lives. The worst official figure that can be thrown at heavy smokers is that they may be said to account for 90% of deaths from lung cancer, although only 1 in 10 gets the disease, many, as we saw in the Introduction, at ages above the average expectation of life. So far from smokers under-rating such risks, Professor Kip Viscusi of Harvard was reported in the *Economist* (20 December 1997) as finding that 'the chances of getting cancer from cigarettes are typically overstated by four or more'.

Does smoking really kill anybody?

After wide reading and deep reflection on the intricacies of rival pleadings, the settled view at which I have now arrived might be briefly stated as follows. Stripping away all the exaggerations of the SS brigade, there is persuasive evidence that heavy smoking is one of half a dozen significant risk factors for cancer; but may be no more *the cause* of that bogus category of 'smoking-related diseases' than the effect of such other individual variables as heredity, diet, lifestyle, social class, location and, on the showing of Professor Hans Eysenck, personality, which he judged uniquely correlated to both smoking and disease.

The clear implication of this formulation is that a crude assertion that someone was killed by tobacco should always be questioned, unless all the 'confounding factors' have been explored. It was along these lines that Eysenck wrote a paper with the challenging title: 'Does Smoking Really Kill Anybody?' It must be acknowledged that he was a highly original and, therefore, controversial figure whom professional colleagues loved to hate. Yet his death prompted an obituarist in the *Psychologist* (November 1997) to describe him as 'the most widely cited psychologist in the world'.

It is for each adult smoker to weigh such risks, along with the other more tangible costs (including heavy taxation), against the less tangible net benefits (struck after setting the discrimination and hassle against the positive enjoyment of calm, comfort and conviviality). To agitated non-smokers still tempted to support various forms of official penalties or prohibitions, I commend the magisterial words of Mill on liberty:

> … the only purpose for which power can be rightfully exercised over any member of a civilised community against his will, is to prevent harm to others. His own good, either physical or moral, is not a sufficient warrant.

Invention of a myth

It was to undermine this powerful appeal to the individual's freedom of choice that 'passive smoking' was invented. Back in 1975, Sir George Godber had addressed the World Health Organisation on the need to go further than frightening smokers about the damage to their own health:

> We must foster an atmosphere where it is perceived that active smokers would injure those around them, especially their family and any infants or young chilren.

Since then, as recounted in Chapter 5, there have been dozens of détermined research efforts to frame smokers as public enemies through 'environmental tobacco smoke' (ETS). Evidence that the findings do not even satisfy their authors is suggested by the ceaseless computer-aided efforts to 'dredge the data', rig the results and come up with new revelations. As we shall see, even by massaging the statistics, selecting the most promising findings, lumping together projects of totally different quality into a mishmash 'meta-analysis' and, in the American EPA report of 1992, changing conventional margins of confidence, no proof has been forthcoming that would satisfy conventional canons of statistical significance. Judith Hatton's exposé is reinforced by my more extensive discussion of the SCOTH report in Chapter 8.

Nor is this failure surprising, since smoke inhaled directly (through the mouth) by the active smoker and then exhaled, becomes much diluted and different in chemical composition from that breathed (mostly through the nose) by the 'passive smoker'. The highly independent *Times/Telegraph* columnist, Barbara Amiel, once reported on a field study which concluded that:

a non-smoker would have to sit behind a desk for 550 continuous hours [say 15 weeks] before being exposed to the nicotine equivalent of one cigarette ....

And it would obviously take longer if the room was larger, the doors or windows were open, and the air conditioning as effective as we hereby invite non-smoking readers to come and judge for themselves in the new FOREST office, five minutes stroll from Victoria station!*

When even the most virulent anti-smoker would have to concede that full exposure to their own tobacco smoke *does not harm the majority of active smokers*, was it ever plausible that in massively diluted atmospheric form it could prove lethal to passive bystanders? It may be irritating or offensive or even, say for some asthmatics, upsetting, but hardly more so than perfume, body odour, garlic or barbecue fumes are for others. Yet millions of pounds of scarce medical resources – financed from charitable and taxpayers' funds – continue to be squandered stubbornly trying to discover even a tenuous link between those two ingenious semantic inventions of 'environmental tobacco smoke' and 'smoking-related diseases'. And when the latest rehash is served up to the press as 'new findings', the television screens obligingly present us with mournful medical apologists who look as though they were hired out to augment grief at funerals.

It is time we looked a little more closely at these professional shroud-wavers.

---

*Audley House, 13 Palace Street, Victoria, SW1E 5HX, Telephone 07071 766 537

8

How wrong can they be?

From my intensive study of the literature over the years, I am left with not the least scintilla of doubt that all the scare stories about 'passive smoking' are no more that the results of militant propaganda disseminated by passive thinking. The tragedy is that it has proved a chronic and highly contagious fever. It is no longer only among excitable Californians that 'passive smoking' has come to be shrilly exploited by relentless lobbyists to persecute smokers at work, in so-called 'public places', and even in private bars. Most cruel of all, this wholly illusory fear has been deliberately puffed up to sow hostility, even hatred, between man and man, and even between man, wife and family. On a recent 'National No Smoking Day', Nigella Lawson deplored that children of parents who smoked were incited publicly in Maoist style to harass them.

Passive rice-pudding eaters?

Rather like the Loch Ness monster, 'passive smoking' goes on rearing its phantom head despite repeated demonstrations of its non-existence. As a whimsical intoduction to the study of facts versus fiction, I commend a report by Nigel Hawkes, science editor of *The Times* (6 August 1997), under the intriguing heading of 'Rice pudding a greater risk'. He recalled that the American EPA had claimed a risk ratio of 1.19 (equated to a hypothetical 19% increase in the risk of lung cancer) for non-smokers exposed to environmental tobacco smoke; and explained that such were the uncertainties that 'risk ratios of less than 2 are regarded as insignificant' and would be dismissed if caused by anything other than tobacco. For perspective, he referred to other studies, including one from Uruguay, which found that:

> ... people who consumed large amounts of dairy products, includ-
> ing rice pudding and milk, were more than four times [=400%] as
> likely to develop lung cancer.

Taking the estimate commonly bandied around that the average
annual chance of non-smokers getting lung cancer is around 1 in
10,000, he reported the risk for 'non-smoking rice pudding eaters'
as 4 in 10,000. The whole question was reduced to its proper
dimensions by an anxious letter from a *Times* reader who did not
eat rice pudding but wondered:

> ... what are my chances if I'm regularly in the same room as
> rice-pudding eaters?

Perhaps a pharmaceutical company will yet come up with a rice
pudding patch to be worn on the arm like scout badges above the
nicotine patch!

In Chapter 3, Judith Hatton makes such a good job of demol-
ishing the contrived scientific and statistical rigmarole of 'passive
smoking' that readers might still ask how academics and medical
practitioners could solemnly put their names to such a fabrication.

Beware of passive thinking

As suggested by my disappointing experience in the House of
Lords, recounted in the Introduction, hatred of tobacco companies
as merchants of death can seriously unbalance otherwise quite
level-headed commentators. But for ambitious professionals faced
with such a hot political issue, it can hardly be doubted that
research funds, publication in professional journals, and official
promotion, to say nothing of knighthoods and perhaps peerages,
are likely to favour people prepared to sign up to politically acceptable conclusions. I can understand readers wondering whether
such self-serving motives could really be sufficient to explain the
strength of the apparent medical consensus against 'passive smoking?' Well, just read on!

The key to penetrating this mystery is that few doctors could
ever find time to pore over a single one of the scores of primary
research reports, let alone of the superficial, almost hilarious,

questionnaires which Judith Hatton exposes for the first time to public view (above, Chapter 3). Indeed, I can't believe anyone else would bother to study them who was not paid well to do so. There is now such a vast outpouring of 'evidence' that even the most conscientious commentators cannot grapple with it. So they fall back on stale second- and third-hand opinion on second-hand smoking! Each time I hear the strident talk about the 'evidence' on 'passive smoking', I recall the words of the 1930s song: 'I danced with a girl, who danced with a man, who danced with a girl,' etc, etc, 'who danced with the Prince of Wales.'

The 'gatekeepers' who control access to politically-correct, ready-to-quote statistics are the wholesalers of reports on a selection of other reports from such campaigning activists as the US Environmental Protection Agency, the British HEA and Scientific Committee on Tobacco and Health (SCOTH) – whose very name has a faintly menacing ring, rather like Expert Enquiry into Bananas and Crime.

SCOTH lays down the law

Just as my co-author and I were putting aside the mountain of documentation on which we had drawn to compile our first draft of this book before Easter, there came to hand – unexpectedly and more or less simultaneously – three key exhibits that taken together finally explode the hot air balloon of 'passive smoking'.

The most prestigious was the report already referred to from the government's Scientific Committee on Tobacco and Health. This runs to 140 pages and comprises a subtle blend of repetitive, dogmatic, superficial, almost journalistic, assertion, combined with acres of technical details, puffed-up appendices, mind-numbing references, and name-dropping annexes. The whole is designed to keep the great unwashed at bay and to dazzle more susceptible politicians with an aura of expert infallibility. The twin purposes appear to be to frighten smokers and create the very 'negative mood states' to which it draws attention, and to fan discord between smokers and their non-smoking fellows.

Before venturing to penetrate the scientific Maginot line around the Committee's familiar array of debatable evidence, I must share with readers a revealing insight on a subordinate issue where my own expertise is superior to theirs. What first struck me as an economist with some knowledge of the theory and practice of marketing was the totally amateur quality of SCOTH's references to tobacco advertising. On reflection, readers might ask: But why should an assortment of scientific professionals (including academics, medical consultants, surgeons, and an authority on gynaecology) be expected to know about such practical matters? To which I reply with a deeper question: Why then should they so far *exceed their terms of reference* ('to advise on the scientific aspects of matters concerning smoking and health') as to lay down the law by recommending – unanimously, of course – annual increases in tobacco taxation and complete, unparalleled censorship of all forms of advertising, promotion and sponsorship?

It cannot be denied that all this was precisely what the Blair government wanted to hear. If SCOTH had left the Minister to invite evidence from qualified practitioners such as, say, Henley Marketing Dynamics International, the simple truth would have emerged that in mature markets like cigarettes (soap, tea, etc), promotion is not concerned with increasing total sales but with contesting market shares between rival brands. This is precisely what tobacco companies have always patiently explained, so SCOTH was bound to be suspicious.

But then how could the commercial innocents of SCOTH be expected to understand that the vociferous lobbying in Brussels for a Europe-wide ban on advertising has nothing to do with a concern for health? It comes from France, Italy, Spain and Portugal, and is motivated by crude commercial anxiety to protect the market shares of their national tobacco monopolies against competition from superior British and American brands.

SCOTH is not alone in falling for the untutored assumption that banning advertising and raising cigarette prices will reduce smoking, despite the weight of argument and evidence on the other side. This exaggeration of the power of advertising comes from failing to accept two facts which hardly require elaborate proof. The first is that youngsters start smoking overwhelmingly in response, not to advertising, but – as research by WHO has confirmed – to the example set by friends and family. The second, requiring a little more reflection, is that the paid messages we single out as 'advertising' constitute no more than the most trifling fraction of the ceaseless, pervasive barrage of information, advice, appeals, warnings and persuasion that daily assail the senses of citizens fortunate enough to live in a free and open society. It may be emotionally frustrating for the SS brigade, but it can hardly be doubted that the piffling £50 million a year spent by tobacco companies on bland brand advertising is completely swamped by the stark health warnings advertised free on every packet, reinforced by the pervasive propaganda and other pressures against smoking. How otherwise would smoking have declined from above half the population in the 1970s to around a third today?

From such tiresome practicalities, two seemingly perverse possibilities follow. So far from reducing smoking further, the advertising ban may lead to an increase – as it has in other countries – by reducing the public's exposure to the exaggerated health warnings, which under the voluntary code take up a fifth of press and poster displays. Incidentally, the ban will also prevent companies from informing customers of low tar content (to which SCOTH, though not ASH, attaches the greatest importance) and announcing such future possible product developments as the so-called 'smokeless' (actually reduced smoke) cigarettes. The second disappointment in store for SCOTH and others is that further increases in the price of cigarettes will encourage both smuggling and legal importation (up to 40 packs of 20 per trip within the EU 'for personal use'), which together supply a growing black market in drastically cut-price (often high tar) cigarettes and hand-rolling tobacco for uncontrolled sale to, among others, under-age smokers. These untaxed imports are already losing the Exchequer more than £1,000 million a year.

Rumbled at last

The trouble with SCOTH is that its members appear no more sure-footed when they return to their proper business of smoking and health. To support their case they look to their expert Committee on Carcinogenity which variously asserts that 'passive smoking' is *associated with many hundreds* of deaths due to lung cancer per year' (p. 83) or *'could account for several hundred* lung cancer deaths per annum' (p. 96). SCOTH's own version was no more precise:

The numbers of people exposed to ETS are not known precisely
but an *estimate would suggest about several hundred* extra lung cancer
deaths a year are caused by exposure to passive smoking. [p. 31,
emphasis added]

This verdict was reached without considering two of the four
largest studies ever undertaken of non-smokers living with smokers, as well as all 18 studies of 'passive smoking' in the workplace
(17 of which showed no increased risk). Its verdict was based on a
risk ratio of 1.1 to 1.3 where, as we have seen, 1.0 would have
meant no increased risk of lung cancer from 'environmental tobacco smoke'. It was thus only after the customary torturing of stale
statistics that SCOTH was able to propagate the simple, stark,
spin-doctor's conclusion that:

Exposure to ETS is a cause of lung cancer and, in those with long
term exposure, the increased risk is in the order of 20-30%.

Even taken as gospel, remember, this increased risk amounts to
identifying – through all the haze of ETS – an increase from an
average annual risk for non-smokers put at 10 per 100,000 to 12 or
13 per 100,000, that is an *additional 2 or 3 victims per 100,000 people.*

Statistical significance?

Unfortunately for SCOTH, their bold declaration directly conflicts with my second exhibit which is no less than the World Health
Organisation's largest ever, ten-year European study of ETS and
lung cancer. Although the full report has, mysteriously, not yet
been published, an official press release in March 1998 – days
before SCOTH – gave the statistical game away.

The study found that there was an estimated 16% increased risk of
lung cancer among non-smoking spouses of smokers. For workplace
exposure the estimated risk was 17%.

Then came the crushing conclusion:

neither increased risk was statistically significant.

This negative verdict on 'passive smoking' from the WHO study reinforced that passed on a similar official Australian report back in 1996 which purported to show that 'passive smoking' caused ten deaths from lung cancer per year throughout a country with a population above 18,100,000. It turned out that this total was created by adding up fractions of single deaths in different age-groups. It recalled the music-hall evidence of PC Plod: 'M' Lord, the lady's body 'ad been cut into 19 pieces, but it 'ad not been interfered with.' A frustrated Australian anti-smoking activist, Simon Chapman, warned that journalists would see the finding as a 'huge joke' and would conclude: '*Official: Passive smoking cleared – no lung cancer.*'

We come now at last to the death knell on 'passive smoking', sounded inadvertently, but I like to think appropriately, in the House of Lords. In response to an innocent, technical-looking question on the epidemiological significance of relative risk factors of between 1.0 and 3.0, Lady Jay, the no-nonsense daughter of the no-nonsense Jim (now Lord) Callaghan, who answered for the NHS, is reported in Hansard (31 March 1998) as follows:

Relative risk provides a measure of the strength of association between a factor and an illness … (for example, if drinkers are twice as likely to suffer from a particular disease as compared with the general population, a factor of 2 may be cited).

A stronger association – *of greater than 2* – is more likely to reflect causation than is a weaker association – of less than 2 – [which] is more likely to result from methodological biases or to reflect indirect associations which are not causal ….

Then, for good measure, she added:

Even when the strength of an association is precisely determined, it is insufficient to confirm a direct causal link between possible cause and an illness.

In officially restating the widely acknowledged rule that risk ratios of less than 2 need to be interpreted with utmost caution and provide no basis for confident assertions of a causal link, Lady Jay dismissed the whole tribe of passive thinkers, who pontificate on the basis of highly-dubious risk ratios of 1.1 or 1.2. What more need be said – except QED!

I invite readers to turn back to Chapter 3, and particularly to re-read Judith Hatton's description of that unrealistic, unanswerable questionnaire (counting partners, jobs, string beans, 'chicken with the skin on', open windows). Then just imagine the kind of anecdotal ramblings which experts treat as evidence and solemnly feed into their heavily-programmed computers to derive empty risk ratios calculated to two decimal places. Finally, reflect for a moment on the plain partisanship of the result-straining, grant-claiming, publicity-seeking cancer establishment, fuelled by the restless itch of some scientists to control how lesser breeds live their wretched lives. Surely, all but the most gullible readers will begin to understand, if not fully to share, our seasoned doubts about the other statistics and analyses that pour forth from such tainted sources. They may even be led to wonder whether tobacco companies – for all their clumsy efforts at self- defence – merit the calumny and hatred routinely heaped upon their heads by the 'scientific' SS brigade.

Who are the 'stooges'?

The *Guardian* recently outdid its usual scandal-mongering with a headline: US TOBACCO FIRM PAID SCIENTISTS AS STOOGES. The supporting story was that in 1988 one company had sought to recruit scientists to act as consultants and to sponsor research projects in order to contest 'passive smoking' propaganda. In like spirit, I might suggest the following headline for a rather more shocking revelation about SCOTH: GOVERNMENT SCIENTIFIC ADVISERS SUPPRESS BENEFITS OF SMOKING. The supporting story might go on to compare the 20 pages devoted to puffing-up 'passive smoking' with a dozen lines, tucked away under 'Miscellaneous topics', devoted to: 'The apparent beneficial effects of smoking on a few aspects of health ....' Bear in mind that this brief, grudging reference to the protective effects against dreaded Parkinson's and Alzheimer's (among other more obscure diseases) relates to *favourable* risk ratios of 2 or more, which implies that *non*-smokers have at least a 100% higher risk than smokers. This excess risk is an order of magnitude higher than the 0.2 or 0.3 (20% or 30%) increased risk on which all the alarm about 'passive smoking' is elaborately constructed.

Too late for SCOTH, *The Times* reported (21 May) on yet another study sponsored by WHO which found that:

> ... smoking may protect against cancer in high-risk women ... The study found the risk of developing breast cancer was halved in those who smoked.

Since that again implies a *favourable* relative risk of 2, it might be thought to warrant interest, if not a positive welcome, from the cancer establishment. But a member of SCOTH was at hand to dismiss the study, despite its publication in the *Journal of the National Cancer Institute*. His reason was that larger studies had shown no such link. The trouble is that precisely the same could be said against the evidence on which he and his SCOTH colleagues relied for 'passive smoking'!

When the tobacco industry is constantly confronted by such consistent bias, I invite readers to ask themselves whether companies deserve to be pilloried by the likes of the highly partisan *Guardian* for seeking support from independent scientists – independent, that is, of the entrenched, world-wide cancer establishment? Bear in mind that any scientists who dare to challenge the SCOTH version risk being ostracised as 'stooges' and even being blacklisted by the medical mafia.

We cannot expect the SS brigade to think again and abandon the search for better and bigger statistics to prove their stubborn obsession that there's no smoke without death. Perhaps the best that can be said of these experts is that they are only human. Having made a large intellectual investment in the bubble of 'passive smoking', and having cast to the winds the scientific watchwords of humility, scepticism and objectivity, few will find it easy to escape the trap described as long ago as 1620 by Francis Bacon in his *Novum Organum*:

> The human intellect, in those things which have once pleased it (either because they are generally received, or because they suit the taste) bring everything else to support and agree with them; and though the weight and number of contradictory instances be superior, still it either overlooks, or despises, or gets rid of them ... that the authority of these previous conclusions may remain inviolate.

No doubt we should all be on guard against straining unduly for evidence that supports our own point of view. But when we fail, the danger of lasting distortion is checked by open competition from the clash of rival viewpoints. The danger arises when experts strain to reach a common position and then collude to impose that opinion on the public and media through the pervasive apparatus of government 'information'. It is this politicisation of science that alone explains the unbalanced debate on smoking, as readers may judge for themselves from the material we have striven hard – yes, perhaps strained – to assemble.

Postscript: Wald v Nilsson

At the risk of appearing to savage a corpse, I must now share with readers the latest study which has just come to hand and which should prove the final interment of any remaining remnants of 'passive smoking'. The meticulous gravedigger is a Swedish professor of toxicology at Stockholm University named Robert Nilsson, who cannot be smeared for any links with the tobacco industry. His 'Working Paper' (dated March 1998) is entitled *Environmental Tobacco Smoke Revisited* and serves as the very model of an authoritative post-mortem on the sorry pseudo-science of 'passive smoking'. What first struck me like a revelation in his impressively documented, clinical critique was that a principal target turned out to be a Professor Wald.

Half a morning spent rummaging through piles of clippings brought to light the report of a TV interview in January 1988 when Professor Nick Wald was quoted as saying:

> Many people are of the opinion that the risk of dying of lung cancer if you're exposed to other people's smoke is something of the order of 10 to 30% greater than if you're not.

Since that happens to anticipate the conclusion of the SCOTH report ten years later, I checked out the membership of SCOTH which confirmed my recollection that Professor Wald's name is, indeed, among them. Not only is he one of the dozen members, but he was the very one singled out to help the Committee prepare an 'updated assessment' of the the relevant literature, which was then paraded as the crown jewels of the whole report. We read that his internal report was duly considered by his colleagues on SCOTH and accepted in preference to a couple of no less independent, scientific assessments that showed no statistically significant evidence for 'passive smoking'. So it came about that, after all the usual technical huffing and puffing, SCOTH unerringly reported a 20-30% increased risk of lung cancer from 'passive smoking'.

Professor Nilsson's modestly entitled 'Working Paper', by contrast, repays the closest attention. It provides a luminously scholarly dissection of the inherent difficulties, discussed earlier by Judith Hatton, in pinning down environmental tobacco smoke – like nailing jelly on the ceiling – and assessing any effects on the health of *non-smoking wives* living with smokers. One snag which alone knocks the bottom clean out of all those precise-looking percentages is summarised under the heading: 'Misclassification of smoker status'. Professor Nilsson patiently explains that outside Europe participants with cancer describing themselves as '*non-*smokers' often turn out under closer examination to be *smokers* in rather large numbers – ranging from under 1 to above 17%. Not that SCOTH's researchers totally ignore such deception. They simply apply a low 'misclassification' rate appropriate to the UK, and claim with a straight face that whether it is applicable to non-westernised populations is 'not known'. In contrast to their strident dogmatism, Professor Nilsson cautiously describes deductions based on such statistical artefacts as 'extremely precarious, if not invalid'.

If this single gaping flaw were not enough to puncture their 'robust' estimates and bury their mountain of computer print-outs on statistical models of 'passive smoking', our cool Swede exposes many others, including biased selection of studies, their variability in quality, the dubious, unverifiable 'recall' of family history and, not least, the inadequate treatment, often total neglect, of 'confounding factors' such as diet, medical history, heredity and ethnic differences.

And what about the absolutely crucial question of the amount of 'exposure' to this supposedly lethal ETS? Professor Nilsson confides that Swedish and UK calculations have put 'high level' exposure as equivalent to smoking between 0.2 and 0.5 cigarettes a day. He quotes a later Swedish study (1996) which recorded ETS in Swedish smoking homes as equivalent to smoking 1/200th to 1/300th of a cigarette per day. It brought to mind an earlier report by three doctors describing an experiment administering chickens with a dosage of some ingredient of 'passive smoke' which was equivalent to a person smoking 'as a very conservative estimate, over 5 million cigarettes each day to reach even the lower threshold limit of response.' But then the whole abracadabra rests on the assumption that smoke is so lethal that there is no minimum level that can be regarded as safe. We are back to the circular reasoning that there's no smoke without death.

It is difficult to doubt that many of the scientific SS brigade are almost professional 'passive fumers' for whom the mere whiff of a naked cigarette is sufficient to affect their customary clinical judgement. I have certainly crossed swords with undoubted experts whose passionate detestation of smoking appears to have rendered them hardly more objective than the most militant of smokers.

Nor, for some at least, is their behaviour wholly irrational, as judged from an economic viewpoint. Under the heading of 'Funding and Publication Bias', Professor Nilsson quotes an American researcher at the National Institute of Environmental Health Sciences:

> Investigators who find an effect get support, and investigators who don't find an effect don't get support.

Nor, alas, do they get publicity – or appointment to government committees! This verdict was recently confirmed by Dr Charles Hennekens of the Harvard School of Public Health:

> Epidemiology is a crude and inexact science. Eighty per cent of cases are almost all hypotheses. We tend to overstate findings, either because we want attention or more grant money.

Back in 1987, Barbara Amiel, an early critic of all fashionable pretexts for political nannying, wrote of 'passive smoking' in one of her forthright columns:

> What I don't like is the lying that accompanies it. The lie is to claim that the health hazards of second-hand smoke have been scientifically established.

More than a decade later, despite all the determined efforts of the health mafia to construct better evidence, that verdict has not been dislodged. Nor will it be, if only because of the inherent difficulties in measuring differential exposure to supected ETS and disentangling the myriad individual circumstances, including the many known confounding factors.

I apologise for having risked trying readers' patience with what may look like overkill of 'passive smoking'. Yet since 1975 this recklessly propagated hoax has enjoyed nine lives, so perhaps it has to be killed off as many times.

If Judith Hatton and I have done no more than nail this particular lie, our hope is that others who have privately confessed their doubts all along, will now be emboldened to speak out. Just imagine the acclaim if a few more truly independent spirits took collective courage to join Professor Nilsson and the other brave spirits quoted here in publicly contradicting that mischievous and mendacious official EU health warning: 'Smoking damages the health of those around you.' The worst that could happen to them would be an immediate routine denunciation as lackeys of the multinational tobacco monopolists – which should at once be discounted as coming from the lackeys of the international cancer cartel!

So take courage. Such empty chastisement might perhaps be followed by a well-earned invitation from Bernie Ecclestone to a Formula One race meeting – so long as the reprieve on sponsorship lasts. Alas, 1998 saw the last of the Benson & Hedges cricket cup final and Rothman's Silk Cut rugby championship.

Keep watching this space

Even as we were putting the finishing touches to this book, signs were multiplying of a long overdue change in the climate of opinion. Hot on the heels of the awkward questions raised above on the SCOTH report, and the devastating US federal judgement against the Environmental Protection (or 'Propaganda') Agency reported by Judith Hatton, a further challenge has been mounted against SCOTH, this time in the High Court. Thus the four leading tobacco companies applied for a judicial review of the report on the grounds, among others, that a nominally 'scientific' committee had rejected evidence without scientific justification; had exceeded its advertised terms of reference; and had failed to consult the companies as had previously been standard practice.

We may imagine the reluctance to take legal action felt by people as vulnerable to public obloquy and political reprisals as those in charge of today's 'wicked' tobacco companies. For decades they had scrupulously avoided confrontation. They had gone out of their way to participate in regular constructive discussion with public authorities on all issues of policy affecting smokers. They were even given to boasting of their long record of co-operation in drafting and enforcing effective voluntary agreements on sponsorship, labelling, tar content, even the ingredients used in tobacco products, as well as on such sensitive aspects of advertising as not appealing to young people and avoiding humour. Indeed, the voluntary code negotiated in 1994 ran to 37 pages and included such serio-comic stuff as:

> Smoking should not be associated with social, sexual, romantic or business success ... In particular, advertisements should not link smoking with people who are evidently wealthy, fashionable, sophisticated or successful ...and should avoid any suggestion of a healthy or wholesome style of life.

Whereas in 1983 Sir Peter Froggatt, as chairman of an earlier incarnation of SCOTH, had gratefully acknowledged:

> a fruitful working relationship with the industry and ... great benefit from our continuing discussions both with the industry as a whole and with individual companies

the current members had produced their latest report without bothering even to go through the motions of civilised consultation.

It was therefore encouraging that on 6 July 1998 a High Court judge conceded the case of the four tobacco companies that SCOTH's report should be the subject of judicial review. The ever-alert Robert Matthews in the *Sunday Telegraph* (28 June 1998) speculated whether the outcome might be the same as in Australia last year:

> where the courts threw out an official report into the health risks of

smoking by government advisers after finding that the consultation process was inadequate.

The best the Department of Health could manage by way of official comment was:

Ministers view the action for judicial review as no more than a publicity stunt.

We shall see! But whichever way the next stage goes, both in America and in Britain, there is at last some reason to hope that the closed season on smoking out the professional anti-smokers may be coming to an end.

Towards the rediscovery of tolerance

Chapter 2 should have already put us on guard against the 'expert', who, the happily non-expert philosopher, Professor Minogue, tells us:

> ... often turns out to be the victim of the most dangerous kind of superstition in the modern world: that which comes garbed in the trappings of science ....

He added with penetrating directness:

> ... we should recognise that doctors and scientists are by no means immune to irrational enthusiasm.

Beware of consensus

Unlike some exasperated fellow-smokers, I have long struggled to believe that at least some medical men who trustingly repeat the well-worn mantra of unrelieved doom and gloom on smoking are innocent of intention to deceive. But then at the independent Institute of Economic Affairs throughout the pre-Thatcherite (and, I might add, pre-Blairite) 1960s and 70s, I witnessed at first-hand the iron grip fashionable fallacies exerted over prominent academics and their political acolytes. With rare exceptions, the most vocal professional economists subscribed with superb certainty to the prevailing consensus in favour of inflationary finance, incomes policy, economic 'planning', trade unions, state industry, 'social contract', and the other sacred cows – right up to 1979 when they were led off to the intellectual abattoir.

Similar collective fancies by other dominant 'experts' intimidated generations of Labour, Conservative and Liberal Democrat politicians to collude in the destruction of traditional education by progressive teaching methods and the spread of welfare dependency by sociological over-indulgence. On the scientific front, we had regular warnings of the approaching exhaustion of global oil supplies, topped-up by a report from the prestigious Club of Rome in the 1970s which predicted that the world would shortly be running out of the raw materials essential to sustain the growth of industrial output and employment.

Even as I write, the obituary columns recount the mesmeric influence of a single guru, the late Dr Benjamin Spock, whose *Baby and Child Care*, first published in 1946, became second only to the bible in world-wide non-fiction sales. Echoed stridently by the predictable chorus of experts, his teachings swiftly became the new orthodoxy. Yet long before he died at 94, he had recanted on much of his earlier permissive gospel which had led more level-headed critics to blame him for 'a Spock-marked generation of hippies'.

For most well-balanced people the inherited corpus of family experience, buttressed by folk law and common sense, preserves us from what Professor Minogue has shrewdly called the 'irrational enthusiasms' of these somewhat incestuous, fashion-prone experts – whether on child care, diet, education, health and safety, state welfare, environmentalism, economic policy and, now, on smoking.

The general lesson I would draw from long observation is that novel panaceas are invariably exaggerated by the media and carried too far by militant activists before the pendulum of moderation reasserts itself. The lesson I have learned is that in place of seeking to impose a fashionable, politically-correct orthodoxy in thinking and conduct, a free society should positively rejoice in tolerating for responsible adults the widest degree of diversity and non-conformity consistent with what non-expert commonsense would recognise as good order.

Perhaps the pendulum is already swinging back, starting from a most unlikely quarter. This year's General Assembly of the Scottish Kirk had before it the report from its Church and Nation Committee which included a gentle rebuke of those criticising smokers who:

... ignore the complex symbolic role of cigarettes as a gift, and a means of sharing and bonding, a ready pleasure and precious moment for oneself.

Well, it's a welcome start, and good news for my haunted Bishop in the House of Lords library!

Beware of 'democracy'

Democracy is too often the pretext for using the coercive apparatus of the state to impose our preferences on others, whether for their own presumed good, or for our own private comfort and convenience, or in the question-begging name of 'the public interest'. The anti-smoking, anti-hunt, anti-car, anti-gun lobbies are driven variously by a mixture of all three motives, spiced with a perverted puritanical enjoyment of stopping the enjoyment of others. The wider the scope of government, the larger the range of individual likes and dislikes that are threatened by the steamroller of this politicised 'democratic' process. Let the SS brigade beware! After smokers, who will be next for the public pillory?

Where the political market supplies prohibitions or favours across the board in response to single issue lobbies or presumed 'majority' votes (remember Tony Blair won a landslide victory with the votes of less than 31% of the electorate), the economic market enables competing suppliers to cater for diverse, even conflicting, minority preferences. Thus vegetarians don't have to lobby against steak houses, nor home owners against renters, nor licensed premises against restaurants, and so on. On smoking, once the divisive phantom of 'environmental tobacco smoke' is blown away, the competitive market would restore the civilised rule of mutual accommodation through the provision wherever possible of voluntarily designated smoking and non-smoking areas reflecting the true weight of private – not spurious 'public' – preferences.

Now that so-called 'representative' democracy has been shown to fall so far short of satisfying the insatiable demands upon it, might we contemplate a return to the original hope for *self*-government? The aim would be to leave individuals with wide autonomy to exercise their own judgement and to accept responsibility for shaping their own lives, enriched where desired by drawing on a dense network of voluntary, local and national agencies for cooperation, mutual aid and philanthropic endeavour.

A boon going far wider than smoking would be to free society from the greatest fraud of party politics, namely the promise that frail, fallible politicians and their scientific bureaucracies can protect us from all risks and relieve us of painful choices and so-called 'quite unacceptable', but often ineluctable, outcomes.

'That kind of liberty'

Confronted with voter resistence to post-war politicians who used to boast that government knows best, Mr Blair and the leading spirits of New Labour have increasingly come round to favour the rhetoric of consumer choice. Few, however, have yet grasped the simple logic that if citizens are to be freer – even free to learn from supposedly 'unwise' choice – politicians must withdraw their tutelary power.

In contrast, on gun control the new government was more restrictive than the Tories, who had in turn been more restrictive than the judicial Cullen Report on Dunblane. On private motoring, the seemingly amiable, Jaguar-loving John Prescott and his political advisers appear to prefer physical constriction and congestion to road pricing; he was even reported as saying that he regards motorists as 'in the same category as hunters, smokers and pistol-owners'. Then we have the paternalistic Dr John Cunningham, who shows no signs of regretting his impulsive prohibition of beef on the bone in response to panic health fears that almost instantly subsided. Meanwhile, on country sports, back-bench Labour Bourbons, like beagles straining at the leash, positively bay for the blood of traditional fox hunters.

And now there's the authoritarian lurch from voluntary restraint on tobacco advertising to the outright prohibition of all forms of promotion, even extending to the monitoring and possible censorship of publications from abroad that might carry adverts of which the authorities disapprove. We have yet to see how far the mutual accommodation of smoking and non-smoking areas will be displaced by the severe discouragement of smoking in whatever the SS brigade chose to define as 'public places'.

Yet the prize of true individual freedom and responsibility could hardly provide a more elevated, potentially unifying – in New Labour-speak 'inclusive' – goal for our mature democracy. It was best articulated by Herbert Butterfield in *Christianity in European History*, where he defines our western way of life as emerging from:

> the growing consciousness, particularly since 1700, that all men – even classes long oppressed and even negro slaves – should be conceded that kind of liberty which gives a larger realm for the exercise of moral decision and personal choice.

Might the approaching dawn of a new millennium provide just the spur for commentators and academics to give a stronger lead to politicians to champion that lofty conception of liberty? In the process we could begin to rediscover traditional British tolerance – on smoking and so much else.

Select Bibliography

Anderson, Digby, et al. *Health, Lifestyle and Environment*, Social Affairs Unit, 1991

Burch, P.J., *The Biological Basis of Disease*, Leeds University Press, 1989

Colby, Lauren A., *In Defence of Smokers!* Frederick, Maryland, 1995

Eysenck, H.J., *Smoking, Personality and Stress: Psychosocial Factors in the Prevention of Cancer and Heart Disease*, Springer-Verlag, 1991

Fisher, Sir Ronald A., *Smoking: The Cancer Controversy*, Oliver and Boyd, 1959

Feinstein, Professor Alvan R., 'Biases introduced by confounding and imperfect retrospective and prospective exposure assessment', in *What Risk?* ed. Roger Bate, Butterworth Heinemann, 1997

Flew, Professor Anthony, *Passive Smoking, Scientific Method and Corrupted Science*, FOREST, London, 1994

Huff, Darrell, *How to Lie with Statistics*, Penguin, 1973

Johnstone, J.R., and Ulyatt, C., *Health Scare: The Misuse of Science in Public Health Policy*, Australian Institute for Public Policy, 1991

Lemieux, Pierre, *Smoking and Liberty: Government as a Public Health Problem*, Varia Press, Canada, 1997

Luik, Dr John C., *Through the Smokescreen of Science*, FOREST, London, 1994

Mackenzie, Compton, *Sublime Tobacco*, Chatto and Windus, 1957

Milloy, Steven, *Science without Sense: The Risky Business of Public Health Research*, Cato Institute, Washington, 1995

Minogue, Professor Kenneth, *Creeping Regulation: Smoking and Citizen*, BAT, 1995

Nilsson, Robert, 'Is environmental tobacco smoke a risk factor for lung cancer?' in *What Risk* ed. Roger Bate, Butterworth Heinemann, 1997

Nilsson, Robert, 'Environmental tobacco smoke revisited', Working Paper, European Science and Environmental Forum, Cambridge, March 1998

Tollison, Robert D., ed., *Smoking and Society* (esp. chapter by Professor Eysenck), Lexington Books, 1986

Voss, Dr Tage, *One Doctor's View*, Peter Owen, London, 1992

Index